Jerry Deans' book is a compassionate and honest look at how individuals become better, stronger, wiser and more content people as they move out of the "wilderness" and into the light of their new deeply transformed life.

A must read for those who need hope inspiration and faith to hold on one more day.

—Carol McDaid
Recovery Activist and CoFounder
of the McShin Foundation and Capitol Decision

There is a difference when speaking with someone who has been through the unthinkable—what they say resonates with your soul. When my wife and I were struck with the unimaginable tragedy of losing our daughter, we needed to hear from people that had been through it. Jerry and Patsi have not only encountered monumental tragedy, but they chose to fight through the ripples of those circumstances to help others. Read this book—for your sake and the sake of those you will be able to walk along side.

—Doug Grote
General Manager, Upward Star Center
Upward Sports

Jerry Deans has a powerful life story of devastating events, personal tragedies, and undeniable recoveries, that he, his wife Patsi, and his family have experienced over three decades. What is so striking is the matter-of-factness of his reporting. Jerry tells the truth about himself, his life, and God. His story is ongoing.

—The Rev. Benjamin P. Campbell, Pastor Emeritus, Richmond Hill

Where is God when your world falls apart? What happens when everything you thought you knew about how God operates is torn to shreds by tragedy? Jerry Deans has experienced devastating loss first-hand, but tragedy does not have the final word. With wisdom gleaned from deep experience and years of study and reflection, Jerry Deans leads the reader to new ways of understanding and coping with the shattering circumstances that inevitably come.

—Joseph Bentz
Author of *Nothing Wasted: How God Redeems What Is Broken*

Jerry Deans has written a powerful story about his personal struggles with grief in the death of a child, his own struggle with cancer and other difficult crises. Throughout his personal struggles, he does not 'sugar-coat' his feelings or mask his dilemma about such happenings, but, nevertheless, affirms the strong faith which underpins his spirit in these dark days. He has been through the 'valley of the shadow of death' and learned to walk with hope and offers assurance to others who face similar struggles. I recommend this book to anyone facing the personal crises of grief or illness. It warmed and comforted my spirit, and I think it will do that for others.

—William Powell Tuck
Pastor, Professor and author of *Facing Life's Ups and Downs, Getting Past the Pain: Making Sense of Life's Darkness*, and other books.

Jerry Deans takes you on an emotional and spiritual voyage through grief and loss. The stories he shares on his journey will act as a compass for others to find their way through their pain, towards transformation and a renewed relationship with God. As I read Jerry's book to my husband, we cried and mourned his losses and ours. Eleven years after the loss of our son, Jerry's book spawned new questions and new conversations that keep the door open for continued growth, continued healing and deeper loving on this path we call life.

—Jo Ann Cockey
Jo Ann Cockey and her husband Tim lost their son Luke to a substance abuse related accident. Jo Ann is a grief support group leader and spiritual director.

Jerry's honest life story and how he survives loss after loss is teaching me how to trust God through the pain of loss. *Lost But Not Forgotten* is full of God's love, full of hope and of healing. A must read for all types of losses in life.

—Brenda Birkitt McEwen
Mom of Johnny in Heaven, 2007
Became widow in 2011

The most current, inspirational recovery experience for the whole family, a real page turner.

—John Shinholser
Cofounder of the McShin Foundation
and the man author credits with saving his son Mark's life.

For anyone who has ever been thrust into the wilderness by life's harshness—all of us sooner or later—*Lost But Not Forgotten* is a survivor's manual offering guideposts, hope, and an eventual way home.

—Joel Blunk
Co-Pastoral Director, Richmond Hill

LOST BUT
NOT FORGOTTEN

How Wilderness Experiences
Can Transform Your Life

JERRY DEANS

Lost But Not Forgotten: How Wilderness Experiences Can Transform Your Life

Print Edition ISBN 13: 978-1-73323-441-2
ePub Edition ISBN 13: 978-1-73323-442-9
Kindle Edition also available

Cover designed by Noah Craig, Dunlap, Tennessee

Interior design, typesetting, and editing by Rick Steele Editorial Services, https://steeleeditorialservices.myportfolio.com

Printed in the United States of America

To my wife Patsi,

We have been co-authors of this book project from its inception. More importantly we have been partners through the ups and downs of life since I met and fell in love with you in 1971. I first honed my skills of writing from the heart when I was trying to convince you to marry me.

You are my best friend.
I am who I am because you draw out the best of me. You have taught me how to love and have convinced me that I am lovable.

I thank God every day for sending you into my life.

ACKNOWLEDGMENTS

This is a book of stories, but how it came to be a book is a story in itself. Many people have been part of making it a reality. Some have passed on and joined the Cloud of Witnesses that the apostle Paul refers to in Hebrews 11.

If you read to the end of this book, you will see that there are over forty people who are mentioned by name throughout, folks who stepped into our lives when we were going through difficulties. Each individual played a part in helping us turn our tragedy into a triumph. Each one followed a mysterious irresistible pull to step up and step in to become part of God's master plan to help us be victorious in the face of great tragedy.

The stories of how that happened are compelling, not because I made them that way but because God inspired those interventions, finished the stories, and called me to witness to what he had done.

Encouragement from lifelong friend Tim Hodges motivated me into preparing what would eventually become this book when he asked me to lead a retreat for the men's group at Winfree Memorial Baptist Church.

Several years passed. Tim died of a heart attack, and I thought that was the end of it until Janie Walker at Richmond Hill retreat center mentioned to me that she wished she knew someone who could lead a grief and loss retreat there at Richmond Hill. I told her that I already had one fully prepared and that Patsi and I could do it. We put it on the schedule and had great response among participants. One of those during the second retreat was Helen Eno Miller, a poet and author who was leader of our centering prayer group. Helen insisted that I needed to put these stories in book form. She organized a critique group consisting of she and Patsy Biggerstaff, also an accomplished writer and poet, and me. Together we trimmed and honed each chapter into a final draft. Without Helen's relentless insistence, the stories would have remained in a retreat format.

Helen helped as hard and long as she was able before her death, and together we decided to submit parts of it to the Blue Ridge Mountain Christian Writers Conference in North Carolina to see if it was worthy of publishing. Locally, dear friend Vallerie King took up the relentless insistence that I should FINISH THE BOOK. I pitched the manuscript to several agents and publishers and signed up for a workshop led by Joseph Bentz. Joseph read part of my work and asked to see the full manuscript. He was very encouraging and helped me to press on in the face of all the discouraging periods of writer's block and turndowns from agents and publishers. Without Joseph's encouragement I would have given up years ago.

Joseph connected me to editor, Jeff Gerke, who offered many excellent suggestions, one of which was that I needed a unifying theme. As I prayed and searched for that theme, I heard Dr Lauren Winner preach a series of sermons at St Paul's Episcopal Church about how Lent is a challenge for us to give up those things that buffer us from the wilderness experiences of life. That resonated strongly with our struggles. Joseph also connected me to another editor, Rick Steele, who saw value in my work and kept me from giving up. Rick connected me to Noah Craig, who helped me design the cover.

So, I thank all of you who have entered into our stories. Thank you, Tim, Janie, Helen, Patsy, Joseph, Jeff, Rick, Noah, and Vallerie, for helping me get this to the finish line.

Now let's see what God intends to do with it.

Contents

CONTENTS

INTRODUCTION

In 2 Corinthians 4:8–9, Paul writes, "We are hard pressed on every side, but not crushed; perplexed but not in despair; persecuted but not abandoned; struck down but not destroyed." The condition I would like to add to that series is lost but not forgotten. My family and I have spent days, months, years, lost in unfortunate wilderness experiences that have been thrust upon us. If you asked me to identify a person in the Bible whom I would like to be compared to, Job, with all his suffering, would be at the bottom of my list. Yet my family endured such a year-long series of disasters and struggles that when a newspaper reporter wrote an article about us, she titled it, "A Man Like Job and a Woman Like Ruth." Here are some of the tragedies she wrote about:

- In July of the year preceding the article, our 16-year-old twin sons were in an accident. One was paralyzed from the waist down.
- One month later, my mother died.
- In December, our oldest son underwent an emergency appendectomy.

- In February, we determined that our other twin in the accident had a life-threatening cervical injury.
- That same day, I learned that I had prostate cancer.

Even before this wave of disasters, our lives had been marked by tragedy. Our sons' accident took place eleven years, almost to the day, from the death of our 16-year-old daughter. Ten months later, we lost our first grandchild, and a short time later, my brother's wife Jorja died of brain cancer.

If the reporter had waited a few more years to file her story, we could have offered her more disturbing material.

2

- In the spring of the year that I now refer to as The Third Siege, one of our sons was arrested and jailed on a charge of felony DUI.
- That same spring, our son-in-law contracted a deadly neurological disease.
- Our oldest son and his new wife went on a dream vacation out of the country that turned into a nightmare.
- Later that same year, our daughter underwent complex surgery for ulcerative colitis and developed complications, which almost took her life.
- In the fall of that year, I was hospitalized for a biopsy and discovered that prostate cancer had metastasized to my lungs.

We've all heard it said that "Whatever doesn't kill you makes you stronger," but having experienced what most people would say is more than our fair share of difficulty, it's clear to me why people are not lining up for these experiences. But the fact of the matter is that if we live long enough, all of us eventually come to a time when pain and suffering take us into the wilderness. And this wilderness is much closer than we think. When that time came for my family, it forced us back to basics, asking the really tough questions about life:

- Why is this happening to us?
- How can a loving God allow this kind of heartache and tragedy?
- How can this possibly be part of his plan?

Even though my wife and I were people of faith and trained counselors, these events drove us into that spiritual wilderness without the skills to survive the journey and no map to find our way back to what we once called "normal." The paths we traveled were strewn with hardships we could not have imagined.

If you have undergone different kinds of tragedy and loss, you already know why I describe them as wilderness experiences. We find ourselves in a place that is desolate and totally unfamiliar to us. We have no previous experiences to guide us through this unfamiliar territory, no map, no handbook, and no survival guide.

In the wilderness, we are faced with problems we have never before encountered, while at the same time we are struggling to get from day to day.

We are ambushed with emotions that come out of nowhere when we least expect them and at an intensity we have never before experienced. Those feelings and our reactions to them bring with them problems of their own.

3

Stripped of any sense of control or notion of well-being, we can no longer convince ourselves that the world is safe and predictable. Overwhelming vulnerability descends upon us like a dense fog, limiting our ability to see clearly. We find ourselves wandering in circles thinking the same thoughts and feeling the same feelings over and over and getting nowhere. We feel alone and isolated, somehow cut off from even our closest loved ones and friends. We want to find our way out of this desolate territory quickly. The sooner, the better. But there is no quick and easy way back. So, we trudge forward with growing despair, searching to find a way out of the wilderness.

But . . . and that one word is the word of power in Paul's description of his many experiences of extraordinary hardship in the scripture I opened with, ". . . hard pressed but not in despair, persecuted but not abandoned, struck down but not destroyed" (emphasis added). And in the case of my family, lost but not forgotten, not alone, not without choices and not without our God, who has promised to turn defeat into victory, death into life.

If we stand on those promises, position ourselves to receive his help, we can be sure that God is doing something creative, powerful, and transforming in the wilderness, even when we cannot see evidence that this process is underway.

This book tells the stories of our journey. It has been a journey of survival, making it through many days when we wanted to give up, and holding our marriage together—against all odds. The destruction in our lives was overwhelming. Oppressed with pervasive feelings of hopelessness, bitterness, and ever-present fear, we could not make sense of the tragedies that had come into our lives, yet we also

4

couldn't ignore the countless acts of kindness from so many different directions. We began to see God, clothed in the likeness of our friends and sometimes complete strangers, pouring out his love, letting us know he was right in the middle of our pain with us.

The many wilderness journeys we have taken opened us to a much larger reality. A power emerged, it seemed, that could only be perfected in our weakness. God's loving, creative presence reached into our fear and sadness. We could not explain how the events that followed our tragedies could have unfolded as they did, except that a loving God, now more our God than ever before, was working to heal us.

This book is different from others you will read on the topic of suffering, in part because of the sheer volume and variety of the tragedy that has beset our family. Moreover, our personal experiences with suffering coupled with my life's work with those struggling with substance abuse, mental illness, and disability, has given me a unique perspective. In support groups and retreats we have led, we listened to the common thread of problems that emerge for all of us when we encounter hardship in our lives. We have also witnessed a wonderful system of healing and resiliency that God has placed in each of us, a roadmap thru the wilderness that is unique to each one of us.

When a virus attacks our bodies, all we experience are the symptoms of the disease. We feel the ill effects, the fatigue, the pain. But at the same time, an army of T cells is marshalling forces to surround and attack the virus cells. An entire command structure, better known as our immune system, is in place determining how best to use the many

5

unseen resources that are available to protect us. Having survived so many wilderness experiences and walked alongside others forced to take their own journey, I am convinced that there is a spiritual immune system, a GPS in each of us that helps us find our way. Patsi and I have witnessed the Master Commander sending out his army of angels, his prayer warriors, and his living saints to keep us from falling and keeping us alive to tell of his love and mercy.

Thrust into the great mystery of suffering, Patsi and I have benefited from a host of experienced wilderness travelers, past and present-day travelers, who grappled with the same questions that confront all of us when we encounter life's hardships. I suspect that many of you reading this book can identify those same people in your lives.

We have emerged with a steadfast confidence that God does his best work in us when we are desperate for him and stripped of our stubborn self-reliance. Our experiences convince us that there are provisions to be found in the wilderness, no matter how difficult our circumstances. The wilderness is indeed much closer than we think . . . but God's love is closer still. He has a plan to help us survive in the wilderness and find our way home. But home is not the same anymore. God gives us an opportunity to replace our emptiness with a closer, more intimate relationship with him.

I have organized this book into three parts. Part I, consisting of the first three chapters, describes the struggle, the chaos, and the disorganization that a loss or tragedy imposes upon our lives. You will learn that despite how disturbing this experience has been for you, what you are feeling and thinking is no different from the necessary suffering we all must endure. I have included a host of practical suggestions that will help you survive the early and perhaps most disturbing stage of a wilderness journey.

In Part II, I shift the focus from surviving to learning to walk through the wilderness. In this section I will share how to recognize the signs that lead forward and the dead ends that keep us in hopelessness. Here we can learn how to deepen our relationship with God even when it is clear that he is allowing great suffering to come into our lives. Believers who suffer, struggle with their view of God, how to pray, and how to trust that God is working in their circumstances. These six chapters will put these age-old issues on the table for consideration. I will share the pathways we have discovered through the valleys of life that endure far longer than we expect and change our lives in ways we cannot imagine.

In Part III, the last four chapters, I explore how God intends to use our wilderness experiences to teach us about ourselves, deepen our trust in him, and transform us to do his kingdom work in a world full of suffering. Our lives will never be the same again, but if we are willing to allow God to teach us and guide us, our stories can give us new meaning, new purpose, and become part of his Master Plan.

Each chapter will begin with questions that you will no doubt be asking, depending upon where you are in your journey. Each chapter ends with a summary of the lessons learned that are universal for that stage of the process.

In his book, Seize the Night, Dean Koontz reflects upon the importance and impermanence of hope:

In this uncertain space between birth and death . . . we need hope as surely as we need food and water, love and friendship. The trick, however, is to remember that hope is a perilous thing, that it's not a steel and concrete bridge across the void between this moment and a brighter future. Hope is no stronger than tremulous beads of dew strung on a filament of spider web, and it alone can't long support the terrible weight of an anguished mind and a tortured heart.

Those of us who have struggled with our own wilderness experiences know how desperately we need hope and how perilous and difficult it is to sustain it on a day-to-day basis. We need to find practical and proven ways to sustain ourselves as we wait upon God to provide his promised comfort and strength. This book will speak to your needs, no matter where you are on your journey. It will help you find your own unique pathway through the wilderness and help you discover how God wants to use your experiences to heal a suffering world.

So, come along with me. Yes, I will share some stories of extraordinary loss. But these stories don't end in the wilderness and are filled with the rich blessing of hope that has been given to us; the hope that prevented us from dying the worst kind of death, the death of our spirits. It is the same hope that can activate your roadmap, your GPS system to recovery, and might be the miracle you have been praying for.

PART I

SURVIVING THE WILDERNESS

How do we survive a tragedy?
What can we expect to experience when
we are driven into the wilderness?
Where can we find help?

HOPELESSLY LOST
AND THE DEATH OF DREAMS

What is it like to suddenly find ourselves thrust,
unprepared, into a wilderness experience?

Grief is the process of facing the death of a dream.
—Marilyn Willett Heavlin

On a warm summer evening, Patsi woke me to tell me that our sixteen-year-old daughter, Shantel, was missing. Earlier in the day, Patsi had taken the kids to the lake at Hungry Mother State Park to swim. One of Shantel's close friends joined them and together they enjoyed the summer sunshine and the refreshing dips in the beautiful mountain lake.

When it was time to leave, Shantel asked if she could stay with her friend for a while. She had done well in school the previous year and had proved herself responsible in all respects. An excellent swimmer, Shantel had achieved her lifeguard certification a few months earlier, and except for some minor knee surgery, she would probably have been working in that capacity somewhere in town. There was absolutely no reason to refuse Shantel's request.

Late that evening, we learned from her friend that she started missing Shantel soon after Patsi and the boys left the Park. Shantel had told her friend that she was going to swim some laps to strengthen her knee. That was the last time she saw her. Most of the day she speculated that Shantel had met other friends and gone with them, without telling her. She stayed around the Park until late in the afternoon, expecting Shantel to return. Then she left the lake to drive around town to find her.

12

As the day wore on, her friend's anxiety turned to panic, and Patsi instantly absorbed this panic when she received the call that evening. When Patsi woke me, I took it as my responsibility to calm everyone down, contact the sheriff and begin to sort things out. There had to be a reasonable explanation.

After learning the facts from Shantel's friend, and spending a few hours at the lake with the authorities, our anxiety grew into overpowering fear. Something was seriously wrong. This was so unlike Shantel. She would not go anywhere without telling us. We quickly refuted the sheriff's hunches based on typical teenage behaviors—that maybe she was off with a boyfriend somewhere, perhaps passed out on drugs or alcohol, or angry with parents and running away from home. The sheriff and his investigator challenged our response that Shantel would not do any of these things.

A surprising number of correctional officers from the treatment center where I worked showed up to support us. These officers were formed into teams to help local authorities search the woods surrounding the lake. As the evening turned to morning, however, and the search parties turned up no sign of Shantel, we prayed that maybe, just this one time, one of the sheriff's hunches might be true. The alternatives were too awful to think about. Patsi was advised to go home, to be there if Shantel returned or tried to call.

Early the next morning, a search-and-recovery dive team was requested. As soon as the team had enough daylight, they began the underwater search. I couldn't believe that Shantel had drowned, given that she was such a strong swimmer. I remembered the day when she was eighteen months old. She slipped away from us and crawled into the deep end of my apartment swimming pool, so, we took her attraction to water very seriously. I spent the rest of that summer teaching her to swim. Even after the near-miss accident, she never feared the water. Swimming was her favorite pastime.

As the morning wore on, I was standing on the beach with one of the correctional officers, speculating whether or not a fish finder he had recently installed on his boat would help with the search. These sonar devices could detect underwater irregularities such as rocks and trees, so maybe it would help us rule out that she was anywhere in the lake.

Then the mood changed suddenly. The divers asked for a body bag. I was stunned. A sickening feeling came over me. I watched as they performed the grim task of loading Shantel's body into the black bag and then into the boat. They kept me a distance away while someone confirmed that it was Shantel.

I had to deliver the news to Patsi. Another officer from the center drove me home in tense silence. Patsi came out on the porch to meet us as we pulled into the driveway. And then I faced a hopeful wife, with the news that no parent wants to deliver nor hear: *They found her. . . . She's dead.*

. . . . .

14   Two years earlier, the leaders of the Department of Corrections chose me to be the warden of a correctional treatment center. My wife, five children, and I moved to the little town of Marion, Virginia. Marion is located in a remote part of the state about one hundred miles southwest of Roanoke. The move was a promotion for me and presented the opportunity to run the one facility that treated mentally ill offenders with the most serious conditions from prisons throughout Virginia. It was a wonderful career opportunity, as my education in Psychology and Social Work, along with my lifelong interest in treatment, would be put to maximum use.

Patsi and I were worried, since this move to Marion would be the second time we had displaced our family in two years. We were mostly concerned about the impact on our children, but not so much about our oldest daughter, Tiffany, who had already graduated from high school. Soon after we moved, she decided to work odd jobs and attend school to become a hairstylist. She was also dating Dwayne, a wonderful young man she met while we were in Chesapeake. Jamie, our oldest son, was seven years old at the time, and the twin boys, Matthew and Mark, were just three. Patsi was a stay-at-home mom and provided the stability they needed in their lives. We were an outgoing family, so we were cautiously optimistic that the boys would manage the move with no problems.

Our biggest concern was for Shantel, our youngest daughter, who was struggling with the delicate teen years. We had previously moved from Powhatan to Chesapeake, and after just one year, moved again to Marion. So, Shantel had been forced to leave behind two groups of friends in a very short period of time.

Shantel quickly dashed our concerns. The assistant warden, Sherman Townley, lived next door with his wife, Jo, and their two boys. Brian and Mike were about Shantel's age. The boys were both star athletes in high school and were doing very well academically. They immediately took Shantel under their wing and introduced her to all their friends. Shantel was gifted in the ability to make friends, and she began to thrive in this close-knit community.

I remember our first parent-teacher conference when one of her teachers commented how surprised she was to learn that Shantel was not a native of Marion. After just a couple of months in town, Shantel had even managed to pick up the accent of her peers. In the next few months Shantel used the move to a new community to reinvent herself. Her grades rose to As and Bs, and she set her sights on becoming an elementary school teacher,

She wanted to apply to Emory and Henry College, only a short distance away and planned to eventually have at least five children.

Some years earlier, Patsi and I made a decision to surrender our lives to God. We joined Powhatan United Methodist Church under Pastor Bill Livermon; a rock-solid man of God. I will never forget his prayer for us when he took us into the Church, "Lord . . . surround this family with a ring of fire and protection from anything that might come against them."

Shortly after moving to Marion and seeing Shantel adjust so well, we felt safe within that ring of fire. We were thriving. Tiffany married Dwayne in the summer of 1986 and moved to Chesapeake. With the help of enthusiastic staff, I identified the potential for the Treatment Center to become a fully accredited, acute care psychiatric facility. Staff were eager to achieve that vision, and we began to work as a team toward that end. Things couldn't be any better. We could clearly see God's hand on our family, and we were confident that we were following his plan for our lives. All was well.

The Ring of Protection—Broken

The ring of fire and protection that had been prayed around my family had suddenly collapsed. Patsi blamed herself for not requiring Shantel to come home with her. I now felt that moving my family to Marion was a terrible mistake. The perfect career opportunity, the wonderful church and community, and the kids' positive adjustment to the small town, had suddenly turned into the worst imaginable nightmare.

16

Friends responded immediately to take charge of our household and surrounded us with a deluge of food, flowers, and phone calls. Tough decisions had to be made that only we could make, and we did our best under the circumstances. We decided that the five-year-old twins were too young to understand what was happening and would be better off staying with friends. On the other hand, we felt that nine-year-old Jamie was too old to be sheltered from the loss of his sister. So, we decided to allow him to stay with us and try to help him cope with the unfolding reality. We felt that to do otherwise might result in complications down the road. A few days later as I stood with him in the funeral home, dressed in his best Sunday suit, tears streaming down his face, I was not at all sure that we had made the right decision. Years later in high school and college, he used the loss of his sister and his anger towards God, to justify substance abuse.

17

This loss set forth a journey for our family that changed all of our lives forever. Marilyn Willett Heavlin authored a book entitled, *When Dreams Die.* She lost three sons before they reached adulthood. Someone once asked her to define grief. She responded, "Grief is the process of facing the death of a dream."

That summer, this horrible grief process suddenly seized our family. It is difficult to describe the devastation that comes with such a sudden and unnatural loss. It crashes into and crushes your life in every way imaginable; physically, emotionally, spiritually. We learned that three out of four marriages do not survive the death of a child. Losing Shantel took us into uncharted depths of sadness and depression we had never before experienced. All of our memories of Shantel turned into gut-wrenching grief.

All of us have experienced nightmares and the relief we feel when we awaken and realize that we have been living in a bad dream. Sudden unexpected losses, like the death of a child, have a cruel way of reversing this process. In dreams, the lost person is suddenly alive and well again. When we wake up, the nightmare, which has now become our new reality, hits us all over again. This goes on for years.

It seemed to us in the first weeks after Shantel's death, that the entire town grieved with us. In a small community like ours, such a genuine response of empathy both overwhelmed us and touched us. We could not believe how people from our church, the treatment center, and complete strangers from the community, were sharing our loss.

We learned something about Shantel in the days following her death that warmed our hearts and yet made the loss even more senseless. Shantel, having successfully found her way into the group of athletically and academically advanced students, was working to bring less popular outsiders into the inner circle. Instead of flaunting her newfound popularity, she had been using it to include others. Kids came up to us to tell us how she had sensed their unhappiness and had begun to work to get them included in her new circle of friends. This information gave us clearer confirmation that Shantel had a gift of love and relationship building. How would she have used those gifts as a teacher and a mother? We can only guess. All of these dreams had to die.

In a very short time after her death, we began to feel alone and cut-off from everyone else, who seemed to quickly go back to their day-to-day lives. A stark new reality intruded upon our lives that stripped away any sense that we were protected from harm. If this could happen once, it could happen again. One evening, shortly after Shantel's death, Patsi and I took the boys for a walk into downtown Marion. They began to pick at each other playfully, and a car sped by as the boys were darting about on the sidewalk. Patsi and I went from calm to panic in a matter of seconds. The bubble of invulnerability most of us live in had been burst, and there was no way to put it back in place.

Events conspired to increase our fear and vulnerability. One year after Shantel's death, Tiffany carried our first grandchild, Brittany, to full term—and lost her at birth. Shortly thereafter, my brother's wife, Jorja, died with brain cancer.

LESSONS LEARNED

As we struggled and stumbled through this experience we began to learn the painful lessons of grief and loss. Over time as we have encountered others who have undergone similar experiences, we have been amazed to learn how similarly we all react to such an assault upon our lives.

The early stages of such an experience of tragedy thrust us unprepared into unfamiliar wilderness territory. Those experiencing tragedy are disoriented in this strange and alien place. Routines that have guided our daily activities become disrupted. Every part of our lives is disturbed. It is difficult to describe how deeply and completely these losses impact our lives and begin to change us. One of the first things to go is our sense of safety and security. Ultimately, we lose our ability to convince ourselves that the world is a safe place and that bad things happen only to other people. Instead of convincing ourselves that we live in an orderly world, we now see danger everywhere we look.

In the beginning, there is a sense that this cannot be happening, that it can't be real. The numbness protects us from the initial impact. We feel like we are floating along in someone else's body. The denial and numbness combined with the initial support from others is a very important helpful factor in the first days and weeks after a tragedy and at the same time it leads us to underestimate the degree and the duration that our lives will be disturbed.

In a very short period of time, that numbness gives way to the harsh reality of the wilderness. We begin to sense that people are withdrawing from us, that they cannot understand what we are going through. Much of the time, support is still available, but we don't know how to access it, and others don't know what to offer. During this period, it is extremely valuable to have a person or persons step in to function as liaison to learn what will actually help and communicate that to others who want to help.

Guilt, shame, anger, and remorse are a natural part of this process, whether or not there is any basis in reality. This leads us into isolation. We look around to see that others are moving on with life. Our lives, in stark contrast, have been altered in ways we cannot even imagine. But there is much work to be done, and to move on as

if nothing has happened will lead to even greater problems. We begin to say what we think others want us to say
instead of being truthful. People of faith begin to grapple
with the questions of how a loving God can allow this to
happen. Those going through the experiences are struggling mightily from day to day and are not likely to know
what will be helpful.

CHAPTER
2

THE PROBLEM
WITH PROBLEMS

What kinds of emotions can we expect to feel when confronted with a wilderness experience? How might it change and challenge our daily lives and our relationships? How does it lead to blaming ourselves and others? What can we expect to think, feel, and struggle with as we encounter the reality of a personal tragedy? How is it changing our view of God and our understanding of his plan for our life?

Life is difficult. This is a great truth,
one of the greatest truths. It is a great truth, because once we truly see
this truth, we can transcend it.
—M. Scott Peck from *The Road Less Traveled*

These opening lines of M. Scott Peck's book, The Road Less Traveled, caught my attention as I searched for something to help us make sense of Shantel's death. I could tell almost immediately that we had been thrust into a dark foreboding territory, and we did not have the provisions to cope with this loss. I couldn't have put it in the words of M. Scott Peck at the time. I simply had a hunger to find some explanation that would account for this unspeakable tragedy.

Many people grieving the loss of a loved one, particularly when the death is sudden and untimely, experience a burning need to know *why*. Those seeking to comfort friends or loved ones try to provide explanations in the face of tragic circumstances. When things are going well in our lives, we probably never stop to ask ourselves why. Looking for answers to *why* seems to be a common symptom for those dealing with sudden loss. Those ministering to people who are going through tragic experiences must be ready to deal with this really tough question.

The simple truth that life is difficult is a good place to start when searching for answers. Dr. Peck explains in his bestselling book that accepting the fact that life is difficult is the first realization we must come to if we are to grow as human beings. When we face a loss, one mindset that interferes with our adjustment is our expectation that life should be easy. When we encounter difficulties, we begin to think something is amiss. It is just one complication out of many we encounter with the problems that come into our lives.

The problems we encounter produce a set of natural consequences, and reaction to those consequences makes the problem either easier or harder to bear. Al Siebert makes a similar point in his book, *The Survivor Personality*. He says, "The way we interact with life events determines how well we survive and thrive. Our attitudes determine our well being more than our circumstances."

As much as we might wish to reverse some life events, we are powerless over the past. But we can learn to respond creatively, no matter how difficult events may seem.

Even if we make the best of our circumstances, we cannot skip over the painful effects that follow traumatic life events. One way our culture teaches us to cope is to be strong . . . put it behind us . . . block out the painful reality that has come into our life. This attempt to avoid the pain involves avoiding feelings and usually compounds the difficulty. It is useful to understand that the symptoms we are experiencing are universal. If we love, pain and grief are inevitable when losses come to us. It is a non-negotiable part of being human.

25

What can we expect to think, feel, and struggle with as a difficult event unfolds?

Grief and Loss Impacts All Aspects of our Lives

Serious illness, injury, sudden loss of loved ones, rape, assault, and similar tragedies, have a substantial and lasting impact upon our lives. After Shantel's death, we had no understanding of how deeply our lives would be affected. Something happened at work, however, that helped me to get clearer about what we were up against. Jim, one of the officers at the correctional treatment center where I worked, was seriously assaulted by an inmate who was being treated for acute symptoms of mental illness. This inmate was also deaf and mute, which made it difficult to communicate with him.

The ward Jim worked in was staffed with only one officer. It was a unit that housed inmates who had been determined to be less dangerous than others. Jim had excellent interpersonal skills and prided himself in his ability to effectively intervene without using force. Unfortunately, his skills were not useful with one particular inmate who was unable to hear or speak.

One day, a serious misunderstanding occurred, and the inmate attacked Jim in a rage. Jim was unable to radio for assistance and the inmate beat him into unconsciousness. If the other inmates on the ward had not stopped the assault, he could have lost his life.

Jim received treatment for his physical wounds and was given some time off to recover. He then returned to work on light duty and temporarily had no contact with inmates. I took the opportunity to talk with him about what he was experiencing as a result of the assault, and he was very forthcoming. He described feeling vulnerable and stripped of a sense of control over his life. Loud sounds or raised voices around him triggered exaggerated startle reactions that left him feeling panicky. Jim was having great difficulty with the experience playing over and over in his mind.

He discussed how confident he had been in his ability to handle situations on the ward with inmates. He felt responsible for the assault, yet he could not figure out exactly what he had done wrong. Worried about returning to full duty, he thought about the attack and reminded himself that if it happened once, it could happen again.

The fact that Jim was so honest with me about his experience truly humbled me. It also struck me that the complications he described closely matched the symptoms Patsi and I had been experiencing since Shantel's death. It occurred to me that if any officers in our circle of influence were assaulted in the line of duty and were dealing with this kind of chaos and disorganization in their lives, we had an obligation to try to help them.

I applied for grant funding to bring in expertise to help our facility develop the capability to assist officers victimized by assaults. We hired a nationally recognized group of consultants who worked in the field of critical incident stress debriefing. In the past, these experts had been deployed throughout the nation to assist in the aftermath of a number of tragic events and accidents from which witness survivors were struggling to readjust.

During our training, I learned that the diagnosis for the symptoms Jim was experiencing was Post Traumatic Stress Disorder (PTSD). They informed us that PTSD was commonly diagnosed in veterans of war as well as a host of others, including rape or assault victims, as well as those who had experienced sudden losses in their lives. It was also common among parents who had lost children.

I began to grasp the seriousness of what my family was facing. This knowledge also provided me with some insight and objectivity into the intense emotional and psychological effects of our loss.

We experienced impact in at least four major areas of our lives; *emotional, physical, psychological,* and *spiritual.* These same impacts reemerged when we went through the loss of our first grandchild and other trials that came upon our family. Previous experience with these symptoms and insight into their cause did not immunize us from their impact as new crises unfolded. But it did help us regain our equilibrium in a shorter period of time. Others we have known over the years describe very similar experiences.

Emotional

In the emotional realm, we often feel fear along with a heightened sense of vulnerability, isolation, and loss of control over our lives. Phillip Yancey writes in his book, *Where is God When it Hurts?*, "Fear is the universal primal response to suffering and yet, beyond a doubt, it is also the single greatest enemy of recovery."

We are hardwired to respond to threatening events with a fight/flight response. Fear and anger are part of that system. Once this system is activated by a traumatic event, it is very difficult to shut it down.

Difficulties and losses require us to face uncertainty. We find ourselves in unknown territory, without a frame of reference to help us problem-solve and no roadmap to help us find our way. Our national reaction to 9-11 is a good example. As a nation, we began to suspect trouble around every corner. Rumors flourished, and the national news media seized upon every indication of danger and additional threat. We experienced fear, vulnerability,

28

hyper-vigilance, and anger. Our personal reactions to unprecedented life events follow this same pattern.

Not long after Shantel's death, a leisurely walk into downtown Marion with our three sons resulted in panic when one of the boys darted into the street as a car sped by. We rushed back that evening to the safety of our home, struck by how an event so benign could produce such an effect.

Some months later, even our home lost its feeling of safety. In a game of Hide and Seek with his brothers, Matthew crawled under his bed and fell asleep. When none of us could find him anywhere, a quiet summer afternoon suddenly turned into panic and chaos, as we searched for him. Throughout the search and hours after we found him, we relived the tragedy of Shantel's death all over again.

We had always tried to be good parents, but now we were thrust into an intense need to try to control and protect our children. This hyper-vigilance was closely connected to painful memories and heartache. Despite our best efforts, we undoubtedly transmitted that intense sadness and fear to our boys.

29

• • • • •

Fear augments and amplifies any pain we might be experiencing, whether it is emotional or physical. Closely associated with fear is the feeling of helplessness and vulnerability. After a traumatic event, we realize that our previous sense of safety and control over our world is nothing more than an illusion. We manufacture it out of necessity in order to protect our mental health, but it is still a fabrication.

When we read about or watch catastrophic events in the news, we may briefly feel helpless or vulnerable. But we move on to the next page or program. Randomness, disorder, and chaos abound in our world, but we would rather not face it. So, we manage to give ourselves some explanation for why a sad incident took place in someone else's life.

When these events crash into our own lives, we are no longer able to convince ourselves that bad things happen only to others. Our bubble of safety has been burst, and it is difficult, if not impossible, to reconstruct. This new sense of vulnerability becomes a troubling companion in our lives.

What do we tell ourselves when a loss or traumatic event comes to us? How do we explain why we have now become the victim? The answer to that question takes us into the psychological realm.

Psychological

Thomas Keating reminds us in *Invitation to Love* and many of his other writings that we do not escape childhood without certain psychological wounds. Even with excellent parenting, we all seem to pick up hurts, disappointments and fears as we are growing up. We usually bury them in our unconsciousness. By the time we reach adulthood, we have worked out certain programs or strategies designed to try to protect us from harm and bring about security, self esteem, and control over our lives. Some of us become very people pleasing and others become very strong and assertive. We intellectualize, using knowledge and information to defend ourselves, or use humor to control our world and those around us. Some become introverted and try to fade into the woodwork. Others use cynicism to keep them from experiencing life's disappointments. Most of us are unaware of these strategies.

For most of my life, I was a survivor, a "worst-case scenario" thinker. The second of two boys in my family, I grew up feeling less competent than others around me. My brother had a three-year head start on me along with a mechanical ability that he inherited from my dad. I felt I never quite measured up to my dad's expectations.

31

Growing up in the lowland tidal community of Poquoson, Virginia, during the years when hurricanes were frequent, also influenced my personality development. I learned to compensate for feelings of inadequacy by always anticipating potential challenges that might be heading in my direction. I became a survivor, staying in a state of mental preparation—my way of dealing with circumstances and controlling life. This guarded instinct had actually served me well as an adult, particularly in leadership positions with the Department of Corrections and the Department of Mental Health. But now, in the aftermath of Shantel's death, it became difficult to relax, since my mental radar was constantly scanning for the next danger or challenge.

· · · · ·

Difficult events introduce a glitch in our programs or strategies for security, esteem, and control. These events resurface and reactivate our old wounds and unresolved life issues. We question ourselves. *Why did this happen to me? What did I do that I shouldn't have done? What could I have done that I did not do? Did I somehow deserve this or bring it on myself?*

The loss of Shantel heightened my anxiety, fear, and hyper-vigilance. My tendency to scan for danger and control every situation clearly was not helping me in this situation. Countless attempts to manage the safety of my family had failed. I also felt guilty that my ambition and hunger for validation had caused me to bring my family to Marion.

Patsi and I were caught up replaying the loss over and over in our minds. It was as if we could somehow change the outcome if we just played it over one more time. I was aware that I was doing this, but unable to stop it. We tried to bargain with the past in other ways. We became caught up in "If only" thinking. *If only I had not sought that promotion. . . . If only Patsi had made Shantel come home with her. . . If only she had stayed a little longer at the beach, she might have been able to save her. . . . If only. . . .*

Physical

As we replay the loss in our minds, we produce the same stress response as the actual event. The fight/flight mechanism is reactivated each time we relive the experience. Our physiology responds by dumping adrenalin into our system. Since we are neither fighting nor fleeing in a physical way, we become stuck in a stress-reaction. The unhealthy biochemical impact on our bodies over an extended period of time can lead to heart trouble, ulcers, headaches, and a host of other stress related difficulties. Dr. Herbert Benson, a Harvard trained cardiologist, has written several books about his research into this process. His first book is entitled *The Relaxation Response*. The relaxation response is the name he has given to a very simple meditative technique that counteracts the stress reaction.

If someone else is responsible for your loss, you may have an additional burden of anger and resentment. If you are responsible, you will experience intense guilt. But even if you are not responsible, guilt seems to be a consequence we all must confront.

33

Trauma, loss, grief, and accompanying stress responses, compromise our immune system and wear us down physically. Our bodies respond to emotional wounds in the same way they respond to physical wounds. Resources and energy are redirected to heal the wound, leaving very little energy for anything else. We are bone-tired with very little exertion and more prone to become infected with viruses or bacteria that are floating around. We sometimes cannot get adequate sleep. At other times, we may need to sleep more than normal. Perhaps we may overeat or have little appetite. Substance use and abuse can be a major pitfall.

Our doctor prescribed a sleeping medication for us after the loss of our daughter. Though it was "non-habit forming," I remember a strong inclination to use it every night. Since sleep was the only way to escape the intense pain, it would have been easy to become dependent. This is why it's so important to have a good primary care physician to work with at this stage of loss. Our physician was reluctant to continue to *prescribe* solutions. And, as former substance abuse counselors, Patsi and I both knew that seeking long-term chemical solutions to this pain was not the answer.

Situational depression accompanies tragedies and severe loss and lingers much longer than we expect. Sometimes professional treatment becomes necessary, and careful selection of knowledgeable professionals is very important.

34 Spiritual

The area of spiritual impact can become a major pitfall for those of us who struggle with loss. It also has potential to help us transcend and transform our life difficulties. As my family dealt with the aftermath of Shantel's death, we witnessed the benefit of being part of a faith community. Members of our church family and community showered us with countless acts of kindness. As people of faith, we could not avoid the very tough spiritual questions Shantel's loss raised for us, and knowing we had a support group of loving friends who shared our faith made it easier to face these questions head-on.

Thanks to my mother, I had been receiving a monthly subscription to *Guidepost Magazine.* Prior to Shantel's death, I enjoyed reading the short stories that detailed God's faithfulness in the lives of people who had faced

life-threatening situations. After Shantel's death, these
stories no longer inspired me. Instead, they angered me
and caused me to question God. If there was a God and
he was all loving and all powerful, how could I explain
what happened to Shantel. Why did he do this to us or
allow it to happen to us? Why did he intervene in some
circumstances, but fail to intervene in ours? Was this punishment for our sins? Friends and acquaintances offered
their explanations: *Well, God needed another angel or babysit-
ter in heaven. . . . Jerry, we cannot understand his ways, but
this is part of his plan. . . . God provides these circumstances to
strengthen our faith.*

Our response to pat answers, however sincere and
well-intentioned they were offered, went along these lines:
*If this is part of his grand plan, then let us out of the plan; if this
is to strengthen us, then give us our daughter back and let us be
weak. How could a loving God do this to his children? Did he
need Shantel in heaven more than we needed her with us? Why
us? Why this? Why now?*

I terminated my subscription to *Guidepost.* No one
offered any satisfying responses to our questions. Despite
the wonderful support we had received from our church
and community, we slid deep into a pit of grief and
depression.

In the fall of the year after Shantel's death, I went to
Washington, D.C., to attend a week-long workshop on
mental health in correctional institutions. For some reason,
I felt drawn to the Vietnam Memorial. A mid-week break
on a cold, rainy afternoon provided me with the opportunity to visit the memorial. Filled with emotion, I stood

35

before names of more than fifty-eight thousand individuals who had given their lives in the conflict and considered the human cost of this effort that had seemed to accomplish nothing in terms of world safety or national security. I thought of the families and friends who were forced to endure the same grief that we were experiencing.

After a period of time, a simple thought came into my mind. It seemed to resonate in my consciousness and bring forth a flood of sadness and tears. But at the same time, it somehow provided relief and resolution to the burning question of "Why?"

"Why not you?"

LESSONS LEARNED

The painful lessons of grief that we were experiencing felt very abnormal to us at the time. Sometimes we questioned if we were slipping into mental illness. What we have learned since then is that these reactions are universal responses to wilderness experiences. What follows are some suggestions for breaking out of the patterns that keep people stuck in grief and stress reactions. Many more suggestions will be included in the chapters that follow.

Most of us have a tendency to underestimate the difficulties that are inherent in moving through life and particularly the experiences of the loss of loved ones, serious illness, or injury, and so forth. Acknowledging that life is difficult creates in us a need to learn, to seek additional information and coping skills. It helps us to focus on a productive learning response to loss and tragedy.

Sudden traumatic events thrust us into a very primal fight/flight stress response and often produce a difficult constellation of symptoms, known as Post Traumatic Stress Disorder. Traumatic loss and the wilderness experience that ensues is difficult to sort out and often requires professional assistance and much understanding and support of loved ones.

Losses of different kinds whether traumatic or not impact us physically, emotionally, psychologically, and spiritually. If we can learn to expect these impacts, we can begin to look for solutions for how to deal with them productively.

One important thing, if not the main thing, to look for when we are going through difficult times is what God wants to teach us about ourselves. What have we been relying on other than him? Traumatic experiences have a way of exposing the survival strategies that we have adopted and those parts of ourselves that we need to surrender to him. As painful as these experiences are, they have the potential to bear great wisdom and life lessons for us—if we can adopt a learning attitude.

CHAPTER 3

STANDING ON THE PROMISES

How will we survive a wilderness experience? Where do we turn to find our way through these seemingly impossible paths we have been forced to walk? How do we distinguish between paths that are dead ends and those that will lead us through this experience? Where will our strength come from when we feel so alone, so weak, and vulnerable? Many are giving suggestions, trying to help. How do we sort through the often-conflicting information? Is God in this with us, and if he is, how is he leading? What is the nature of the help he is offering?

Blessed are those who mourn,
for they will be comforted.
—Matthew 5:4

No matter how deep the pit . . . Gods love is deeper still.
—Corrie ten Boom from *The Hiding Place*

In the fall after Shantel died, the visit to the Vietnam Memorial in Washington, D.C. and the questions that came into my mind, were significant. *Why **not** you*

Jerry . . . What makes you so special that you would somehow be beyond the reach of the bad things that happen to the people in this world? I remember doing a mental calculation of the number of grieving family members represented by each name on the Memorial. Hundreds of thousands had been forced to deal with sudden death. How could I expect that we would somehow be spared that same kind of loss? It struck at my self-centered belief that God would always protect us from harm.

At that time, we had no idea what we would have to do to dig out of the devastating grief and sadness that had taken over our lives. But the question that came to me at that memorial shocked me into an important new reality. *We were not the first who had experienced this kind of loss and we would not be the last.*

40

If you have ever been in the wilderness then you know that it is dark and discouraging. Tragic circumstances and loss take a terrible toll on our lives and all of those around us, ushering us into a whole new painful reality. Our world is turned upside down, as our lives seem to be spinning out of control. We experience confusing feelings and emotions, and we begin to question ourselves and our faith while wondering if God has abandoned us. Circumstances have changed our lives forever. There is simply no turning back to the way things used to be—no matter how hard we work to resist change. The comfortable predictability we've enjoyed for so long no longer exists, and we don't know where to turn for help. We look around and see that others have seemingly returned to their lives, yet we feel alone and isolated.

The psychological strategies that we have taken on to protect ourselves from harm and discomforts have failed, leaving us feeling vulnerable and confused. Richard Rohr, in *The Authority of Those Who Have Suffered, Breathing Underwater,* and *Falling Upward,* speaks eloquently about how suffering destabilizes our ego and strips away our over-reliance on ourselves. As long as things are going well, we believe that God is overseeing things on our behalf from a distance. Relying on our self-made system for coping with daily problems, we *feel* as if *we* have things under control. I would have denied it at the time, but at some level I believed that my good fortune, my promotions, and my beautiful family were all rewards from God for giving my life to him and a credit to my hard work. Shantel's death did not fit into the story of my life up to that point. At first, I was confused and angry with God. Then I moved into despair and depression. If God was not protecting us from this kind of harm and suffering, what good was a relationship with him?

The bad news is that the wilderness is deeper, darker, and more complicated than we think it should be. The pain is more severe than we expect. It takes longer to heal than we think it should. Much longer. So, we also have to contend with our own personal expectations. First, we get down, and then we get down on ourselves for getting down.

What do we do to get out of the wilderness? Where can we turn for help? Do we let the anger and blame we feel toward God separate us from him when we need him most? Is God's love deeper than the deepest pit? This was not part of my self-made story. But if I would only allow it . . . consent to it, God was about to take my story, even this tragic ending to our daughter's life, and make it part of his story.

Another event occurred, in the fall of that year, which offered us clear direction. It was an annual worship service at our church led by members from the congregation. In this particular service, several people spoke about what the church had meant to them during difficult times in their lives. Two of those who spoke, James and Eula Moore, described what it had been like to lose their son, Jimmy, in a motorcycle accident a few years earlier. They thanked the church for the overwhelming support that was given to them after his death. As I listened, it occurred to me that we desperately needed to spend time with people just like James and Eula; people who had lost children.

After discussing this with Patsi, I contacted our pastor, Fred Austin. He immediately began to contact all those he knew in town who had lost children. In just a few weeks he brought them together to meet with us, and from there we decided to start a monthly support group. In the first meeting Fred began the discussion by saying that he could not imagine what we were going through and he had no answers for many of our questions. He simply wanted to be present to learn from us so that he would be better prepared to help others in the future. We have learned over the years that many pastors are very uncomfortable with the really tough questions and feelings that come up in this kind of group. Fred showed great courage and love by being willing to participate with us and not feel like he had to come up with all the answers to our questions.

At first, Patsi and I found it difficult to share the feelings we had been experiencing. Our emotions were so overwhelming, we were only able to cry and listen to the other parents. In the few months following Shantel's death, we had bottled up our feelings. We started to worry that what we were experiencing was abnormal, maybe even mental illness. The group shared with us that they had all experienced the same feelings, behaviors, and questions. Some of the members had seen grief counselors after their losses. They assured us that it was all part of our "new normal."

Each meeting was painful. Many tears were shed, as we left each meeting emotionally and physically exhausted. We often wondered if the sessions were helping or hurting us, but we knew we were surrounded by loving people who understood. We were astounded that others were willing to relive the pain of their losses to help us. When we tried to thank them, they assured us that they were receiving as much as they gave.

Gradually, we no longer felt as lonely and isolated. As we discovered that others had experienced similar feelings and reactions, ours lost much of their sting. We came to realize that we were on a wilderness journey that none of us would have chosen to take. But we were not alone on that journey; we had traveling companions who were willing to encourage us and show us the way.

Over the next few years, the support group became our lifeline. We learned many lessons that helped us recover from the loss of Shantel and helped again years later, when our family faced other trials. What follows in this chapter are a few of those lessons.

43

Let People Help, but Choose Wisely

We learned from the group that we needed to sort through the help offered. One by one, the group members recounted examples of hurtful and insensitive things that had been said to them. Well-intentioned people who had never been through similar losses, seemed to need to provide tightly-wrapped theological explanations. They usually implied that our tragedy was part of God's plan and even though we could not comprehend it, he knew what he was doing.

These explanations trivialized our loss and added to our confusion. They suggested that because we were believers, the pain or sadness we were experiencing was not necessary or would go away quickly. We would have been even less forgiving, except that many of us recalled having been guilty of offering the same superficial explanations in our earlier attempts to comfort others. We began to understand the intention behind this less-than-useful help and move past the anger and complicating questions it raised—learning instead to listen to those people who had lived experience with loss and take what others had to say with a grain of salt.

Some people from whom we expected support and help were simply not present. We learned that it is important to avoid investing time and energy trying to figure out *why* they were absent. We learned to accept that some people are not competent helpers. Few in our society learn how to support others during difficult experiences. We suspected that our loss somehow raised issues that they would rather not face.

There were others however, who had never experienced similar losses, but *were* able to be present with us. They seemed to understand that they didn't need to have the answers to all of our questions. They were simply willing to be in the pain and share it with us.

We met people who were not dealing effectively with their grief, years after their loss. At a training event, I met a man who had also lost his daughter. Since we had this tragedy in common, I was eager to talk to him about his experiences. However, not far into the conversation, I learned that he had given up on his faith and that his wife had left him over his drinking. We met other couples who had become separated or divorced after losing a child. The evidence that most marriages don't survive this loss frightened Patsi and me. At the same time, it made us more determined to beat the odds.

Choose to Get Out of the Ditch and Do the Work of Grieving

A year or so after our support group began meeting, our pastor, Fred, arranged for a day-long workshop with Elizabeth Brown. Elizabeth lost her daughter some years earlier and wrote a book to share her experience with others. One point she made that day struck me like a lightning bolt. Only a person who had walked in our shoes had the legitimacy to pose such a question to us.

Each of you has the best reason in the world to get down in the ditch and wallow in the sorrow of your child's death for the rest of your life. No one would blame you. You would be fully justified. But the question is this: If

45

you make that choice, would you be honoring the life of your loved one? And is that who you are?

Elizabeth was able to confront us that day because she herself had stood at that fork in her road to recovery. She was not suggesting that we should deny the painful reality of our loss or avoid the feelings we were experiencing. She was pointing to a temptation that is part of the journey of recovery. Each of us has to turn away from the tendency to stay in a state of hopelessness and take on the permanent identity of a mourner, cancer victim, assault victim, or whomever. I refer to this as a temptation, because it is powerful and seductive. It provides justification for anything we might be inclined to indulge in; overeating, overdrinking, self-medication . . . name your poison. I found myself at that decision point with Shantel's death, and years later, when we were confronted with other trials. Jamie, our oldest son, became aware in his early twenties, that he was using Shantel's death to justify his substance use.

For me, there was also a temptation to avoid the feelings I needed to face. Returning to work after Shantel's death was difficult. I had previously found my job challenging and rewarding, but suddenly it lost all of its importance. Concentrating on daily problems was difficult and sometimes impossible. I particularly lost tolerance for the ongoing "people problems" that are part of every workplace. I lost the fortitude and energy I needed to do the mediation, which was my rightful role as the facility director. I found myself overflowing with anxiety and a confused mix of feelings.

46

One day, I felt a need to take a trip out to the lake where Shantel lost her life. Once I was alone on the beach, the memories and feelings of the search and recovery quickly took over. The grief that I had been suppressing in order to get through each day rushed to the surface, and tears flowed. I found this experience exhausting, but at the same time I felt emotionally cleansed. Clarity returned to my thinking, and I became aware of how blocking my grief interfered with my ability to do my job. I resolved to come back to the lake on a regular basis. For me, the lake became a sacred place to spend time with God, particularly when I was feeling troubled and anxious. It was a milepost in my wilderness journey and became an important place to go to help me experience the feelings that my daily job required me to set aside. Finding spaces and time in our lives to let go and fully experience our pent-up feelings is all-important. This is particularly true if you are male and have been programmed to avoid sorting through your feelings, no matter how helpful the experience can be.

Patsi, on the other hand, could not go near the lake for many years without feeling ill. Her role as a stay-at-home mom now proved to be counterproductive for her recovery. Each day, after she sent the kids off to school she found herself at home surrounded with all the memories of Shantel. While I had to set aside time to allow myself to release my feelings, she was alone in her sorrow and grief every day. Eventually she decided to take a job as a social worker on the admissions unit at the mental health institute. It was a fast-paced work environment that forced her to set her feelings aside to get the job done. It was exactly what she needed.

The grief support group and the workshops we attended, helped us see that we needed to allow each other to grieve in our own unique ways. A major source of conflict, sometimes ending in divorce, is that spouses often expect their mates to grieve the same way they do. One of the resources we discovered along the way pointed out that there is, within each of us, a God-given road map to healing. The map is different for each individual. The work of grief requires each of us to figure out our own pathway to healing.

Stop Digging

Winston Churchill is quoted as saying, "When you find yourself in a hole, stop digging!" One of the most important parts of our grief work is to identify the personal mental patterns that keep us stuck in the ditch of our sorrow. It is even more important to choose an alternative. One of those mental patterns is unforgiveness.

Cindy Freeman, the choir director at our church, lost her sister, Carla, and her niece, Jenny, in a car accident in Wytheville, a town just north of Marion. A truck driver fell asleep and ran them off of the road, killing them both instantly. Her parents, Henry and Sylvia, joined our grief support group. As we listened to Henry recount the details of the accident, Patsi and I began to realize how fortunate we were that we had no one to blame for Shantel's death. Henry and Sylvia had the pain and sorrow of losing their daughter and only grandchild. But Henry, in particular, had the extra complication of resentment and unforgiveness to deal with. While Patsi and I struggled with *why* Shantel's life was taken, Henry knew exactly why his daughter and granddaughter lost their lives. It was one man's negligence—an African American man. Henry suspected, but could never prove, that the driver was using drugs to try to stay awake. The driver's company attorney instructed him to never make contact with Henry or Sylvia, which further frustrated Henry.

Henry had not been raised to be prejudiced. However, this loss caused him to not only despise this particular black person, but his hatred spilled over to all black people *and* all truck drivers. Even the fact that Henry's own brother was a truck driver did not stop his overwhelming anger. Bitterness had overtaken him so much, he exceeded the reach of anyone in our grief support group. Hatred and unforgiveness became a major obstacle to his healing and consumed him. He would lie awake at night, caught up in thoughts of revenge that were totally out of character for him.

49

But God provided a way for Henry, even in the midst of his hatred and resentment. During the years that our support group met, Henry held on to one other person's experience. An elderly woman who attended our group lost her son to murder. The person convicted of the murder threatened to kill her when she was released from prison. Henry marveled at her perseverance. Over and over he said, "If she can survive this . . . then I can." She became Henry's role model. Finding another person who has survived a loss like your own and who can share with you how they did is extremely helpful. And Henry did survive, but the resentment and unforgiveness lingered. Remember Henry. I will share more about how God worked in his situation to heal that unforgiveness in a later chapter.

Turn *to* God or Turn *Away*?

Finding ourselves in the wilderness, each of us must decide if we will do the work that the experience requires of us. Will we remain stuck in the painful and predictable sorrow of what we have lost? Or will we *stand on the promises* . . . his promises, and cry out to him for help? Jesus says in Matthew 9:17, ". . . no one pours new wine into old wineskins." If we choose to rely on him, we have to let him be who he is—not who we have imagined him to be.

I struggled with the *ring of fire and protection* that had been prayed around us when we joined the church years earlier. My belief that God would protect our family from harm wavered. God had new wine for me, and I needed to let him reveal himself in his way and his time. I had to reach the point of surrender. It was an uncomfortable place to be, particularly since I had convinced myself up to that point that I was in control of my life. Now it became clear that I was not in control and had never been. This was one of the important lessons that God wanted me to learn.

It also became clear that God was in the pit with us. We saw evidence of his love in the people who had immediately responded to us following Shantel's death. In time, we began to sense that we were on a journey of recovery, and a loving, compassionate presence was guiding us. He led me to the Vietnam Memorial to help me see how many others were on the journey. He provided the grief support group to give us the permission to experience the feelings and sort through the confusing grief reactions. He provided the right job for Patsi at the right time; the right words from Elizabeth Brown at the time when we needed to choose recovery over despair. As others in the community had losses, he helped us to just show up and share their sadness.

The pain of our loss continued long after we expected it to be over. But gradually we stopped asking God *Why?* and started asking *What now, Lord?* Even though we could not begin to see how God could use our loss, we began to believe that somehow, he would.

51

LESSONS LEARNED

I conclude this chapter with a summary of the lessons we learned and have witnessed others learning as we have walked with them on their journey.

Wilderness walking (and survival) is much more complicated, more difficult and lasts longer than we can possibly imagine. We find ourselves on paths that do not lead to recovery and we have to learn to double back to find our way.

We come to forks in the road where we must choose who we will be going forward. Will we take on a victim identity and stay in the wilderness with anger, bitterness and blame or will we do the work that is required to grieve and grow?

It is important to seek help from seasoned travelers but at the same time we must choose wisely. Anyone who offers quick fixes, or shortcuts and has not done the work that the wilderness requires should be approached with caution.

During times of great difficulty in our lives, we begin to learn the true value of a relationship with the Living God. It is important to acknowledge and give thanks for the evidence of God working in our experiences. In our need and desperation, he becomes more the source of our strength than ever before.

PART II

LEARNING TO TRUST GOD IN THE WILDERNESS

How can we maintain and deepen our
relationship with God even when it is
clear that he is allowing great suffering to come
into our lives? How must we change our view of
God in order to recognize his presence and
leadership in the wilderness?

CHAPTER
4

WAITING ON THE LORD

Once we find our way through one tragic wilderness experience, we tend to think that our bad luck is behind us. How do we make sense of why we are being revisited with tragedy? What have we learned from previous journeys? How has our previous experience taught us which paths to avoid? Where are these experiences leading us in our walk with God? How must we change our view of God in order to recognize his leadership and guidance in the wilderness?

> *. . . But those who wait on the Lord shall renew*
> *their strength. They shall mount up with wings*
> *like eagles, they shall run and not be weary,*
> *they shall walk and not faint.*
> —Isaiah 40:31 **NKJV**

Eleven years after the loss of our daughter, unbeknownst to our family, we were about to be driven back into the wilderness. The year started off with a number of trials that were not outside our realm of expectation. Six years earlier, I had taken the position of Director of Southwest Virginia Mental Health Institute which was down the street from my previous position at Marion Correctional Treatment Center in Marion, Virginia. My new job provided a great sense of satisfaction, but it also produced a significant amount of stress on any given day. Six years after I took the position, my mother was 93 and living independently in her home in the little town of Poquoson, on the coast of Virginia. In April of that year, she suffered a fall and was not bouncing back as quickly as we had hoped.

Patsi and I left our 16-year-old twins, Matthew and Mark, with some friends and traveled to Poquoson to help my brother arrange home care for Mom. When we returned to Marion, we learned that the boys had been accused of shooting out some streetlights and windows with a BB gun. By the time we were able to get the boys to come clean with us and the investigating officer, we learned that the Commonwealth's Attorney intended to make an example of them. So, we decided at that point to hire an attorney to defend them in court. We had hoped to handle it informally by having them apologize and earn the money to pay for the damages.

For a number of years during the week of the 4th of July, we had been vacationing in Alabama with Patsi's relatives. Given the troubling family events of this particular year, we were really looking forward to the family vacation on Lake Mitchell, where Patsi's Aunt Dean and Uncle Dale had a cottage. Some of the most relaxing and peaceful days in my memory were these summertime visits. This one, by all appearances, would be no different . . . at least it started out that way.

On the afternoon of July 3rd, I was out on Lake Mitchell on a jet ski. For about an hour or so, I circled the creek. Then I decided to turn the engine off and just drift along to soak up the sights and sounds of the wildlife on that beautiful summer day. I was about as relaxed as I was ever able to get at that time in my life. All the worries about Mom, the job, and the boys' legal problems, had drifted away. Patsi and Aunt Dean were back at the cottage working on a quilt. Uncle Dale was taking a nap. We were all looking forward to the family cookout and reunion the next day.

Matthew and Mark had ridden with their cousin Mandy and two other teenage friends to Montgomery to pick up Mandy's car from the dealer. They had stopped off in Clanton and called to tell us they were heading back to the lake to join us.

Then the storm broke and thrust us back into another wilderness experience.

One of Dale's friends met me in a boat as I headed back to the cottage. "Jerry, hurry . . . follow me . . . the kids have been in an accident"

"Are they OK?"

"One of them is OK. The other one is still trapped in the car! Come, I will take you to them!"

He drove me to the scene of the accident. Four of the kids were lying on the road, being checked out by emergency workers, bloody and bruised, but not seriously hurt. There were flashing lights, ambulances, and police cars. About thirty people gathered, including Patsi, Dean, and Dale. They told me they had been working about forty-five minutes trying to free Matthew from the car, which was about sixty feet down a ravine beside the road. As I arrived, they were bringing him up on a stretcher attached to a winch. He was pale, but alive and conscious.

Uncle Dale looked at me and said, "He can't move his legs."

We rode to the Clanton Emergicare Center in a Coosa County ambulance that felt as if it might fly apart at any moment. After Matthew was X-rayed, I could see pain and concern on the faces of the doctors and nurses. They had confirmed that he had some feeling in both legs, and they began to talk in terms of "some hope." They were going to transfer Matthew immediately to UAB Hospital, Alabama's premier medical teaching facility in Birmingham.

We rode at speeds up to 95 mph on Interstate 65 through dense holiday traffic to the UAB Emergency Room.

All along the way, I cried out to God, "Please don't let this be happening . . . It can't be as serious as everyone thinks it is. Let this be a dream that I will wake up from!" "Lord . . . Where is the peace that I am supposed to feel? Why am I terrified? Where is my faith?"

After several hours in the UAB Emergency Room with our family gathered, the chief resident came to the waiting room to speak to us. He described the injury and gave us the preliminary prognosis.

"The chances that your son will ever walk again are not one in a million, but they are not 50/50 either."

We weren't ready to hear what he had to say. We were still in shock and denial. I could not get past the panic to think of how to pray.

Matthew had sustained a very serious compression fracture of his spine right around his waistline. After hear-

58

ing this, Patsi and I were scared to death, but we remained hopeful. We knew nothing about spinal cord injuries.

Matthew was young and strong. Just one month earlier, after only his first season of track and field competition, he had placed 7th in the Mile at the State Championship in Lynchburg. We could not begin to grasp the significance of this injury. People told us that UAB was one of the best places in the nation for dealing with this type of injury.

On Saturday, the 4th of July, we waited through surgery and recovery. Family gathered with us in the waiting room, and everyone was hopeful and encouraging. None of us fully understood the nature of the wilderness experience we were facing.

We were told that surgery went well. The neurosurgeon and orthopedic surgeon were able to realign the bones in Matthew's back and install metal rods with screws and hooks. The X-ray of his back looked like a Christmas tree, with all the instrumentation that had been installed.

The next morning, two things shocked us into reality. The orthopedic surgeon came by and told us that the chance of Matthew ever walking again unassisted was very slim. Optimistically, with the help of leg braces and a walker or crutches, he might get upright again. It was more likely that he would be in a wheelchair for the rest of his life.

Just moments later, a phone call came to us from Pam Slemp, a friend from our home church in Marion. We talked for a long time about how her brother Mike, a quadriplegic, was injured and what life had been like for him over the last twenty years. It was only then that the full impact of Matthew's injury hit us—and it left us completely stunned.

It was now becoming clear that this was no afternoon thunderstorm that would come and go quickly. This was a massive hurricane of life-changing proportions. On a Sunday afternoon while all over America, people were wrapping up their holiday weekend, it was just beginning to hit us that Matthew would never run the mile again or play soccer. He might never climb stairs again. I remember Patsi saying, "Oh Lord . . . ! You know we don't even have a house that Matthew can come home to." All three bedrooms and our two bathrooms were on the second floor.

Some days later we realized that the therapy and rehabilitation planned for Matthew were not planned with anticipation of helping restore functioning, though function might return. It was simply designed to help him learn to manage his condition; to do transfers from his bed to his wheelchair and from wheelchair to car seats. As the rehabilitation doctor described it, rehabilitation was to learn to "play the cards he had been dealt."

I'd like to be able to say that I never once throughout this experience doubted God or wondered, "Why us Lord? Haven't we already had our share of heartache and tragedy?" This seemed like such cruel irony. Our Fourth of July celebrations for the past eleven years had been flooded with the memory of Shantel's death. The loss of our daughter, granddaughter, and sister-in-law, in such a short period of time, had been devastating beyond our imagination. But we dedicated ourselves to healing, and with the support of friends and a loving God, we found

the strength to move forward. We even convinced ourselves that our bad luck was behind us. After all, the number and succession of losses we had experienced were rare.
The odds were now in our favor, right?

So, eleven years, almost to the day, after losing Shantel, we were not prepared for this major storm that came
crashing into our lives. But, ready or not, we were thrust
into the midst of another horrible family tragedy, another
wilderness experience.

I remember getting very angry with one pastor who
visited Matthew. He told us that if we believed, the healing miracle would happen. But he warned us that if we
had even a particle of doubt—that doubt would block the
miracle. By then I knew hundreds of people were praying for us. I could not believe that God would go poking
around in all that intercession for us and say, "Well, too
bad, Jerry has some doubt. I guess I will just have to move
on to the next case." I could not accept that the God I
knew and loved would do such a thing.

Most of us surround ourselves with a veil of invulnerability. That veil had been stripped away from my family eleven years earlier. So, we found it very difficult to
approach Matthew with miracle thinking. Should we say,
"Son, we know you are going to beat the odds. You are
going to get the miracle cure! We know God will not let
us down." There were those who took this approach with
us, but it didn't ring true with me nor Patsi. We both had
doubt, and we knew that if we did not get the miracle,
Matthew might break himself on that kind of hope. How
do you split yourself in situations like this? How do you
prepare yourself for the worst and hope for the best?

61

Waiting on the Lord...

Now, our particular circumstances may be somewhat unusual, but the dilemma I have just described is not. Is it? We have all had storms of one sort or another strike our lives, and we have all struggled with how to pray. Do we pray for and believe in the miracle? What do we do with the doubt we feel? Once our bubble of invulnerability has been burst, we realize that bad things **can** happen to us, and not just to people who bring it on themselves. At that point, we have a new set of questions to answer about the nature of the universe and God. These events strip us of our false sense of control.

Think about it for a minute. Do you believe that God protects you from physical harm providing that you seek his will and live your life according to his plan for you? If you have not experienced a control-stripping event in your life, you might say "Absolutely! . . . God is in control! Nothing happens to us without his will and consent."

Others might say that such an idea is childish or wishful thinking. After all, God willed his own Son to die on the Cross, so why would he protect us from harm? He often sends harm into our lives to fulfill his purpose. Is that your idea of a loving God?

If you have had random tragedy strike you or those you love, you are forced to revisit your beliefs about God. If God is all-powerful and all-loving, how do you explain the tragedy and heartache that is so prevalent in our world?

Some will try to comfort you by offering that the event is God's will. Was it God's will when our daughter's life was suddenly and tragically ended? Did God somehow cause Matthew's injury to occur in order to accomplish some greater good? We could not accept that a loving God would do such a thing. Many people have said to us, "God must have a reason for this." Many of us are confused about how God does and does not act. When things are going smoothly we don't have to confront these questions. But, when tragedy strikes, we are thrust into the really tough questions of life.

When the storms of tragedy come into our lives, our sense of justice and fairness is challenged. We begin to personalize events and start to ask the universal questions: *Why? Why me? Why us? What have we done to deserve this?* Our problems are then complicated with our answers to those questions. As described in chapter two, we also find ourselves impacted by the cascading emotional symptoms and secondary problems that follow tragedies. To say the least, our worldview is turned upside down, and many of us need to revisit our personal theology. Ironically, these disruptions come at a time when we are least able to think clearly.

63

The events of July were only the beginning of our family's problems that year. In August, my mother died. In December, our son Jamie underwent an emergency appendectomy. The following February, we found out that Matthew's twin brother Mark had a serious but previously undetected injury from the July car accident. That very same day, at age 50, I was diagnosed with prostate cancer.

LESSONS LEARNED

This new wilderness experience brought with it an education of its own. The following are some of the lessons we learned that may be useful to you.

If we have previously experienced a traumatic life experience, it does not lower our odds for additional tragedy. Our name goes back in the hat, and we are just as likely to experience random hardship as the next person. This is a tough pill to swallow.

But if we have spent some time in the wilderness, and we have worked to learn the lessons the wilderness teaches, we have internalized growth that we may not know we have, even though the circumstances of the difficulty may be very different.

64

Successive trips into the wilderness will provide us with opportunities to draw closer and closer to the living God, if we are willing to seek him with our whole heart and surrender our rigid view of how God acts in our lives.

CHAPTER
5

A MESSAGE OF HOPE

Hope: What difference does it make in our ability to survive a wilderness experience? How does prayer work when we are struggling to find solutions and direction during periods of darkness?

'Tis a fearful thing to love what death can touch, a
fearful thing to love, to hope, to dream, to be and oh to lose.
A thing for fools this, and a holy thing...
—Yehuda Halevi

Matthew's accident was on July 3rd. He had surgery on the 4th, and on the 5th we woke up to a whole new terrifying experience of spinal cord injury. Fresh out of ICU, the first thing we encountered was Matthew's propensity for pressure sores. When he was still a little boy I gave him the nickname Green Frog because his skin was so soft and moist. Now, in just forty-eight hours he had developed sores on his heels. Pressure sores for spinal cord injured patients can be deadly, so we had to learn how to deal with them. The doctor ordered special boots which prevented his heels from touching the bed. These boots had spurs that could be extended to keep his lifeless legs upright.

Then we learned of the potential for deep vein thrombosis, the medical term for life-threatening blood clots—one of the many side effects of spinal cord injury. Daily heparin shots were required to thin his blood. When nursing assistants arrived to transport Matthew to get X-rays of his back, we learned that spinal cord injury affects blood pressure. The first time we tried to get him upright, his blood pressure dropped to dangerous levels, and we had to put him back in bed. They gave him morphine for pain, which sapped his energy and caused fitful sleep and constipation. It was clear to us that he was experiencing depression, a side effect of the morphine, but also resulting from the sinking realization of his new circumstances.

On the sidelines the family stood by, helpless and shocked. We watched him go through this pain and suffering and wondered how he would handle it at age sixteen, how we would all have to change our lives to meet these new challenges. To say that he was down and out was an understatement. We watched him deal with the realization that he had gone from peak physical condition to not being able to bathe himself or even roll over in bed without assistance. His muscles began to atrophy from the waist down, and his whole body weakened more each day he remained in bed. What would we have given to see him get back some sense of control . . . to see his spirit and sense of humor return. . . ? Just about anything.

Breaking into this new reality was a man named Leland. Leland was one of the nurses on Matthew's hospital ward. But if I could have chosen from all the nurses who were rotating care on that ward, I would have put Leland at the bottom of the list. As I watched him work with other patients, I saw that he was loud and boisterous, and I quickly judged him to be arrogant and unprofessional. Leland was African American, and he looked like he belonged on an NFL team instead of a hospital ward for children. His arms were as big around as my thighs, and his sleeves were rolled up, it seemed to me, just to punctuate the size of his muscles. His neck and shoulders were huge. I hoped he would get pulled to another ward or go on vacation so that we would not have to deal with him.

Close up, Leland was another story entirely. Matthew had been assigned to the Children's Hospital because the hospital staff did not want him to be exposed to the negative attitudes that were characteristic of many adult patients. But Matthew was over six feet tall and now 145 pounds of dead weight. It took four or five of the women staff to move him from his bed to a stretcher or wheel chair. So, after observing these assistants struggle to transfer Matthew back into his bed, we began to question the decision to keep him with children. That is, until Leland showed up one afternoon, as several staff were struggling to transfer Matthew from his wheelchair back to his bed. Leland ordered everyone to step aside. He proceeded to pick up Matthew single-handedly as if he were a ten-pound sack of potatoes and laid him gently back in his bed. At that point, I was thankful for Leland's size and physique.

67

But Leland had another characteristic that made him invaluable for our situation. Leland was a *born-again, believing-attitude, specialist.* The first night he was assigned to Matthew will be forever etched in my memory. Soon after he introduced himself, and before he knew anything about our religious leanings, he witnessed to us in a powerful way. Remember that Matthew was at his lowest and needed something that none of us was capable of giving because of the shock we were all experiencing.

In a calm voice that filled the room with peace, Leland said:

A few years ago, before I understood what I was dealing with, strange physical sensations would come over me. The hair on my arms and neck would stand up, and I would be overcome with tears and a sense of peace and love. An old man that I knew at the time told me that I was experiencing the Holy Spirit. Now that I am a Christian, I know that what he told me is true. But what I want you to know is that when I walked into your room tonight, I experienced those sensations as strongly as I have ever felt them in my life. You must have a bunch of people praying for you, because this room is filled with the Holy Spirit. Look...

And Leland stretched out his arms for us to see the hair standing up.

Leland knew immediately how to engage Matthew's sense of humor, and, in a matter of minutes, he had Matthew rolling in laughter. Matthew was seriously constipated from the injury and the effects of the morphine. Leland *insisted* that they we going to get Matthew broken

68

loose and cleaned out on his shift! He was going to be personally offended if Matthew pooped when he was off duty.

I quickly moved Leland from last place on my evaluation of nurses, all the way to number one. The encounter with Leland was one of the first tangible signs that God sent to us, in the midst of the chaos and fear that followed Matthew's injury. It was a foreshadowing of the many blessings that he had in store for us. Morphine erased Matthew's specific memory of what Leland said to him that evening. But Matthew recalls, "Leland was like an angel in disguise. He made me think that if I had faith and trust in God . . . everything would be OK." Leland, like the angels in the Bible, brought a *message of Hope.*

When people shared with us that their churches had been lifting us in prayer, I assured them that we were experiencing the impact of that prayer in ways that they could not imagine. And so many people prayed—churches all over east, central, and southwest Virginia, Churches in Alabama, Tennessee, and Indiana. Every day we learned of others who had spread the word to their relatives and loved ones across the country. Several pastors and lay representatives took our needs to their district and annual conferences. We had no doubt that the people praying for us numbered in the thousands.

To be at the center of so many prayers was an extraordinary experience. And God responded with extraordinary results—results so remarkable that many years after the fact, I am compelled to share the stories of how he worked in our situation. God's presence was conspicuous. He was in this with us, and not just holding our hands saying,

69

"there, there . . . everything will be okay." He was moving, touching, inspiring, activating, transforming, and dragging us along, completely amazing us in the mystery and wonder of it all.

We first saw the answer to prayer in Matthew's attitude. His spirit and strength quickly returned. In just a couple of weeks, Matthew was exceeding every goal the physical therapists set for him and amazing all of us with his wonderful sense of humor. As painful as it was for us to see Matthew disabled, our previous loss helped us to see that his injury was nothing like losing a child. Matthew was still Matthew. We all began to focus more on what we had rather than what we had lost. Cards and letters started coming to the hospital; so many that at one point the person in the mail room stopped in to say that he *just had to see the **celebrity** who was receiving all the mail.*

Matthew was discharged from Children's Hospital and continued his outpatient treatment at the Spain Rehabilitation Center, one of the top rated spinal cord injury centers in the nation. He and Patsi lived with Aunt Dean and Uncle Dale in Clanton and commuted to Birmingham, which was about an hour's drive. This outpatient arrangement allowed Matthew to receive world-class rehabilitation but avoid the negative peer pressure from the adult patients that so concerned his providers. Mark also stayed in Alabama to support his brother. He worked for his Uncle Dale in his construction business.

Dean and Dale provided much needed love and encouragement. They also had specific experience with the rehab specialists in Birmingham, experience they had gained as they raised their daughter Sabrina. Sabrina had lived with Spina Bifida from birth and had undergone rehab from numerous surgeries at the hospitals and rehabilitation centers in Birmingham. She also had a wheelchair van that she allowed Patsi and Matthew to use for the commute to the rehab center.

Dean bought Matthew a Siamese kitten he named Mister Myagi. Myagi was delighted to ride along in Matthew's lap everywhere he went and provide him with the unconditional love that only a pet can give. In some respects, given the injury he had sustained, Matthew couldn't have been in a better place.

But Patsi and I were seriously overloaded. Our house was inadequate with all of our bedrooms and bathrooms on the second floor. A decision to sell or renovate had to be made before Matthew could return home. My mother was struggling with end-of-life issues in eastern Virginia and died just one month after Matthew's injury. Patsi was completely caught up in Matthew's care; turning him in bed each night every two hours, watching for pressure sores, helping him toilet, bathe, and dress, and transporting him back and forth to Birmingham each day.

On another front, our son Jamie had stopped attending classes at Virginia Tech. We had serious concerns that he was in a downward spiral of substance abuse. During this time, Patsi was sensing that Mark had an injury more serious than his doctors had discovered.

Under normal circumstances, Patsi and I considered ourselves to be competent to handle the daily stress associated with being parents of four children and carrying

71

out my job as director of Southwest Virginia Mental Health Institute. But these were clearly not normal day-to-day stresses. It took everything we could muster to get through each day. I found myself crying out to God as I traveled the seven-hour drive back and forth from Marion to Clanton, trying to hold my family together and maintain enough focus to earn a living.

LESSONS LEARNED

As difficult as it is to look to God with hope and faith when events are dragging us down, that posture helps us to see how God is working in our circumstances and opens us to see his movement in our situation.

72 Hope is a powerful catalyst. It activates our inner guidance system to healing and recovery. Hope comes from unexpected places and people once we look to God for it.

There are times in life when it not only rains—it pours. Asking for prayer and learning how to surrender control to God are sometimes our only options. The deeper the need, the greater the opportunity to experience God's loving mercy.

CHAPTER 6

TRUSTING HIS LOVE AND GOOD WILL

How do we position ourselves to receive the help that God wants to send into our lives? How do we identify the dead-end paths in our wilderness journey? How do we learn to lean on God and begin to embrace the negative and painful circumstances that come our way?

Never be afraid to trust an unknown future to a known God
—Corrie Ten Boom

have heard it said that *you never know that God is all you need until you find yourself in a situation where God is all you have.* Recent circumstances took us well beyond our ability to deal with life. It was not a wholly unfamiliar place for us. We had experienced the same sense of helplessness after Shantel's death. But we knew God loved us, and we had already settled a lot of the questions that emerge when such an event comes into one's life; *Why us?*

What have we done to deserve this? Is this punishment from God?

We knew that there is no guarantee of protection from circumstances and that sometimes, bad things and random tragedy happen to good people through no fault of their own. We also had learned that blaming God or ourselves was a dead-end street and a temptation we had to avoid in order to look for his action in our circumstances.

So, we continued to ask for prayer from everyone we knew, and we looked to God for answers. We had learned that faith is not a feeling. Faith, in our experience, is a conscious choice to stand on his promises. It is an act of will to believe that God will make a way even when we feel fearful and confused and can see no way forward.

And we quickly began to see evidence of God's response to our needs.

The first day I returned to work after Matthew's injury, I opened up my desk drawer and found an affirmation that I had copied from one of the Christian growth series sponsored by our church on Wednesday evenings. The affirmation came from a book entitled *Beyond Ourselves,* by Catherine Marshall, and reads as follows:

> I trust the good will and the love of my God. I open my arms and my understanding to what he has allowed to come to me. Since I know that he means to make all things work together for good, I consent to this present situation with hope for what the future will bring.[1]

1 Catherine Marshall, *Beyond Ourselves* (Grand Rapids, MI: Fleming H. Revell, 1994), 94.

The relevance of this note, and how it came to me so soon after the accident, *struck* me. It brought such peace that I kept it in my billfold. As I traveled back and forth on weekends, I pulled it out and reread it. The more I considered it, the more I became convinced that every word of it was perfectly suited for our situation. I examined it line by line and asked myself if I really believed what it said.

Jerry . . . do you really trust the good will and love of your God?

Reflecting back on the previous eleven years, we had witnessed countless examples of his love and good will. Patsi and I had slowly but surely emerged from grief and depression. With the help of a grief support group, our relationship with each other had not only survived, but was stronger than ever. Love and affection flowed freely in our family. We had learned not to take our time together for granted. We were thankful for our church and community. We often said to one another, if it was ours to lose a child, it could not have happened in a more loving, supportive community than Marion.

We had settled in our minds that our God did not cause our daughter's death. The idea that God could do this would be completely inconsistent with the love we had witnessed from those he had moved to support us. We had experienced the emergence of a special sensitivity and desire to reach out to others who were dealing with losses. So, we could see that God intended to work through our life experiences to help others—even through the death of our daughter.

75

The challenge to us now was to trust him again, surrender our weakness to his strength, and *consent to this present situation with hope for what the future would bring.*

The first time I came home after Matthew's injury, I
only stayed for a few days before returning to Alabama. I
called Helen Burkett, who was a dear friend, a member of
our church, and also the real estate agent who had sold us
our house. I explained to her the problem with our house
and asked her if she could help us sell our place and find
one with at least one bedroom and bath on the first floor.
She said that she would contact other agents and start
looking around town to see what was available. When I
returned the next weekend, Helen called and said:

"Jerry, you don't have to sell your house. The church
is going to help. Duncan McGregor is presenting it to the
missions team, and we are setting up a Matthew Deans
Fund. James Moore has offered equipment and materials
at cost and donated his company's labor for any heating
and air conditioning you might need."

I was floored. "Helen, . . . We can't ask the church to
do that!"

"Jerry, trust me," she said. "The church needs to do
this as much as you need it to be done."

At the time, our church was experiencing some serious
internal problems. There had been major differences of
opinion. In my way of thinking this would not have been
the time to call on the congregation for help. But God
saw it differently. For him, it was perfect timing and the
confirmation of that began flooding in.

The following weekend I stayed home for the first
time since the accident. I began to hear about all who had

volunteered their services. Bill Huber, architecture and design work; Bill and EP Ogle, construction; David Dixon and Freddie Williams, electrical; Bobby Coe, plumbing; Lloyd Vicars, Mike Guy, Charlie Edmiston, Duncan McGregor; the Slagels, the Browns, the Creggars, the Chislers, the Hauvers—the list of volunteers and contributors went on and on.

I will never forget the day I signed off on the building permit as "Contractor." Growing up, I learned a lot of skills from my father, who was gifted mechanically and also quite proficient in a variety of other trades. Carpentry, however, was not one of the skills I had picked up from him. I must have slept through those lessons because I couldn't even build a respectable doghouse. So, it was comical, if not ludicrous, for me to sign on to provide oversight for the design and construction of a handicapped addition to our house.

77

But God was clearly leading others who did have the skills to respond, so I trusted and obeyed. And we witnessed a wonderful plan unfolding. Harry Howe, a minister who runs a local mission project, came over to our house to survey the situation. He said that he could do the foundation work, but he could not get to it for a couple of weeks, and he didn't have any earth-moving equipment to take down the trees and dig the footers. That afternoon, Rick Richardson a local dentist called and invited me to come to supper. Kevin Harman, a licensed contractor, came up to me after supper and said, "Jerry, I want to help with your addition."

I asked him if he knew anyone who had earth-moving equipment for trees and footers.

"Yes, I have them."

"Great . . . When would you be able to start?"

"Right away. . . . When do you want me to start?"

The following Saturday, the first time we needed labor to help dig the footers, doubt crept over me. *Do people really want to help? Will they really have the time?*

A scripture flashed through my mind; *Ask and you shall receive. . . . Knock and it shall be opened unto you.* So, I picked up the list of those who had volunteered to help and made only two calls. Jay Harper responded that he could come in the morning and Charlie Sturgill was available in the afternoon.

Sunday morning Gene Cleveland, our church lay-leader opened up the service with scripture from Matthew 7:7-8, *"Ask and it will be given to you. Seek and you will find. Knock and the door will be opened to you."* What an interesting "coincidence".

The day we were laying block for the foundation, Betsy Brown stopped by and offered to get lunch for everyone. The same thing happened another Saturday with Mary Slagle. Evenings when we would work until dark with nothing in the refrigerator to even warm up, Sylvia Richardson, or Shirley Chisler, would stop by with a meal. About the same time someone on a particular day would have to leave, someone else would show up to fill in. Many but not all of those who helped out were members of our church. Others were co-workers or just folks from our community who heard about our need.

There were friends like Don Chisler who stuck to us like glue throughout the entire project, and there were

78

others we did not even know who provided a particular skill at just the right time. Someone, whose identity we still do not know, cut my grass all summer while I was traveling back and forth to Alabama. One morning when I opened the door of my car to drive to work, there was an anonymous envelope containing one hundred dollars on my seat. It was simply labeled *For the Matthew Deans Fund.*

Whenever there was a day when we needed help, that help would show up in just the right numbers, with just the right skills. On one Monday evening when we were framing and needed a lot of assistance, fifteen people just dropped by. I remember coming home, some evenings after working late, and not being able to find a place to park my car.

What amazed us was that there was no one person or group of persons orchestrating this incredible convergence of skills and resources. At the end of the week, our pastor, Jim Pollack, would stop by for a few minutes, or call to ask about the status of the project. On Sunday morning, he would make a quick announcement about the kind of help needed at the Deans' house. That was the extent of the coordination, and yet it all came together in time for Matthew to return home that fall.

When it was completed in the winter, it consisted of a nine hundred square foot wing, designed to match our house. It included a handicap-accessible bedroom, living area, closet, and bathroom with enough space for Matthew, Mark, and Myagi. Hugh Slagle and Gene Hendricks, two retired church members, finished it off with a ramp connecting our driveway to our back porch, which now provided the entrance to the new addition.

Matthew returned to a hero's welcome. He had responded extremely well to the specialists at the Spain Rehab Center, but we were concerned that the care he would receive in rural southwest Virginia would not measure up. However, Terrie Blankenship, who worked in the physical therapy department at our local hospital, adopted Matthew and dashed our concerns with her love and enthusiasm. With her help, together with the care he received from the Spain Rehab Center, he achieved about eighty percent return in one leg and just enough in the other leg to lock his knee and walk upright.

One year after his injury, Matthew and Patsi returned to visit the orthopedic surgeon in Birmingham who had operated on Matthew. Matthew walked into his office assisted only with a cane. The surgeon asked Patsi, "Did you tell him what I told you, that he would probably never walk again?" Patsi replied that we had not. He examined Matthew. Then he turned to the resident physician he was supervising and said, "This is why you should never tell a person with spinal cord injury that they will never walk again. Matthew . . . you are a walking miracle!"

The prayer and support that we received produced something else that no amount of rehabilitation could accomplish. Matthew's attitude throughout the experience was more amazing than the physical return he received. We had been warned, from the beginning, that once the reality set in, Matthew would hit an emotional brick wall, characteristic of those with spinal cord injuries. That never happened in his case. We are convinced that his attitude was a direct result of the prayers and the knowledge that so many people were supporting him.

LESSONS LEARNED

This was an extraordinary experience with incredible answers to prayer. However, imbedded in our experience are lessons for all of us.

It is important to not complicate the disorganization that a wilderness experience brings to our lives by blaming ourselves or God. These dead-end paths become clearer when we have had previous wilderness walking experience.

Learning to open our understanding to what God wants to teach us positions us to wait expectantly for his help and movement in our lives.

The more challenging the circumstances and the more desperate we are, the more needy and open we can become to draw upon God at a new and different level.

These kinds of situations are where God does his best work. This is why we are blessed when we are poor in spirit.

I cannot overstate the strength of the principals imbedded in the affirmation from Catherine Marshall that I found in my desk that came to me at the beginning of this experience.

I trust the good will and the love of my God. I open my arms and my understanding to what he has allowed to come to me. Since I know that he means to make all things work together for good, I consent to this present situation with hope for what the future will bring.

Fully trusting God's love and good will is such a simple statement, but it is the place we must start. For most of us, we only learn this incrementally—after we have been stripped of our self-reliance many times and witnessed how God has worked to lead us through the wilderness experiences. The extent that we doubt God's love and good will for us blocks us from being able to open ourselves to the present circumstances and God's action.

Opening ourselves to what God has allowed to come into our lives requires that we embrace our situation even though we do not agree with it and cannot fathom why he has allowed it to happen. This mindset cuts through the blaming and bargaining. It also creates a space in which we can remember to draw strength from past experiences through which God has led us.

The final step in this process is to look forward with hope and expectation for what God will do in this instance to send his vast resources into our lives to meet our needs. This means we can live without fear and anxiety based on the conviction that God truly is in control and somehow, someway, he will work whatever he has allowed together for good (see Romans 8:28).

CHAPTER 7

THE VALLEY OF
THE SHADOW OF DEATH

What challenges can we expect when we face a life-threatening wilderness walk? When we are thrust into a personal fight for our lives, how do we keep our minds clear and our hearts open to God's leadership? How do we break the consuming power of fear over our lives?

But reach out and take away his health and he will surely curse you to your face. All right, do with him as you please, the Lord said to Satan. But spare his life.
—Job 2:5–6 NLT

Get a physical. Something is wrong in your body. Get a physical!

Where did that thought come from? I did not have time to get a physical. There were too many other things to be concerned about. How would we afford this addition? Where would we get the skilled labor to build it? How would Matthew adjust to this injury? Would he lapse into a state of hopelessness and depression like so many other spinal cord-injured patients? Was I giving enough time to the job? God, help us! I can't juggle all these priorities.

Get a physical. This is very serious. Your family depends upon you. You **must** take the time to get a comprehensive physical!

I was in good health. No problems since that surgery four years ago for diverticulitis. Up until Matthew's accident, I had been exercising regularly. I was only fifty years old. I didn't have time to get a physical.

Get a Physical!

That summer and fall, I struggled to balance the stressful job of hospital director together with the construction of the house addition and the weekend trips back and forth to Alabama to see my family. I felt stretched well beyond my capacity. The sixteen-hour round trips provided ample opportunity for stress and worry—and a lot of prayer. It was during these trips when I was alone and quiet, that the persistent thought came into my awareness that I needed to get a physical.

I first shared this persistent leading with Patsi, and then I called Dr. Paul Brown, who, in addition to being our family doctor, had become a close friend since we had lived in Marion.

"Paul, I don't know where this is coming from, but I have had the strongest leading I have ever felt in my life that something is wrong in my body and I need to get a physical."

"Come on in, Jerry. We will start with blood work and give you a thorough check up."

84

After the blood work results, Paul called and told me everything looked good. Cholesterol was a little elevated but nothing to be alarmed about. All other results were within normal limits. My prostate-specific antigen (PSA) was 2.23 which was about average for a man my age.

So, I returned to the seemingly endless issues that confronted us as a family and tried to put aside the message that something was wrong in my body. But the same premonition persistently returned. Patsi, who has always been a very intuitive person, was sitting in a waiting room one day and noticed a magazine article by Katie Couric, who had recently lost her husband to colon cancer. She called me at work.

"Maybe it's colon cancer. You had that surgery a few years ago to remove part of your colon. Maybe you should ask Paul to set you up for a colonoscopy."

Paul responded to my request and quickly arranged for the test. The doctor who performed the procedure reported that everything in my colon looked normal but during the test she felt a nodule on the right side of my prostate gland. She referred me back to Paul for further examination. Paul repeated the digital rectal exam but could not find the nodule. He pointed out that my PSA was well within normal limits for a man my age. But, he concluded, if I wanted a tiebreaker, he would be glad to refer me to a urologist. I was determined to get to the bottom of this persistent leading and decided to go for the referral.

The urologist retested my PSA and the measurement had actually gone down to 2.13. But he also repeated the digital rectal exam and felt the hard spot on my prostate gland. He arranged for a biopsy.

It was now seven months after the twins' accident. Matthew was back at home, receiving physical therapy from Smyth County Community Hospital and physician follow up from a spine specialist from Bristol.

Mark had been experiencing persistent neck pain, but examinations had not revealed any significant problem. Patsi's intuition told her otherwise, however, and she insisted that Mark be examined by the same doctor who was treating Matthew. X-Rays, MRI's, and physical exams were conducted, and we awaited the results from these tests, while at the same time the result of my biopsy was pending. On Friday, Mark was scheduled for his appointment to review the results of his tests. That same afternoon, the urologist called me with the outcome of the biopsy.

"I'm sorry to have to tell you this, but the biopsy revealed cancer in four of the six samples we took from your prostate gland. You have bilobal prostate cancer. Come in Monday for an appointment and bring your wife."

I left work and met Patsi in the waiting room at Smyth County Hospital, where she and Mark had just seen the spine specialist. She told me that the doctor had diagnosed a hyper-flexion of Mark's C5 and C6 vertebrae, which, if not corrected, presented a serious risk of paralysis from the neck down. She said that she had somehow known that Mark had a serious injury. I shared with her that I finally knew the reason for the persistent leading to get a physical. I had prostate cancer.

We were not surprised with either of these diagnoses; in fact, we had been expecting something serious in both cases. Now that our intuitions had been confirmed, we were thankful to know what we were up against. Nevertheless, we were also battle-weary and anxious about the future.

The coming together of these two diagnoses on the same afternoon, seven months after Matthew's injury, which took place almost exactly eleven years after Shantel's death, overwhelmed and disturbed me at the deepest level of my being.

I was stunned emotionally and spiritually. When friends and loved ones learned of these additional trials, they just shook their heads in disbelief. We had just experienced some of the most powerful evidence of our lives that God loved us. But when would this onslaught end? We felt as if we were under siege. How would we deal with these new trials?

Mark had been pushing past the pain, working with Uncle Dale in Alabama, and on the house addition with all the volunteers, and playing varsity soccer at Marion Senior High. Thank God, he was not paralyzed as a result of a fall on the job or a collision on the soccer field. The hyper-flexion was treatable, and we quickly scheduled surgery.

Matthew was progressing well. In fact, he had received some return of feeling and control in his left leg and was beginning to experience an additional small amount of return in his right leg.

But now my life was on the line. The urologist had misgivings about surgery and suspected that the cancer had penetrated the prostate gland. If that was true, I was dealing with metastatic disease, and surgery would not be the best option. In addition, it was possible that I was dealing with a rare but deadly cancer that produced smaller amounts of PSA. Rather than giving me a clear treatment recommendation, he vacillated and put the decision back on me. What was all his training for if not to give me a clear course of action to take?

He suggested that I meet with a radiation oncologist. This specialist spelled out the treatment process and was willing to proceed, but he also was not sure that it was the best option in my circumstances.

I explored the web feverishly and found out that some prostate cancers are slow-growing and don't result in death. Others are aggressive and life threatening without treatment. If metastasis occurs, it eventually ends up in the bone, and death, when it comes, is often very painful. Some swore by radiation; others recommended surgery; still others were recommending radioactive seed implants. All alternatives came with risks of side effects: incontinence, impotence, radiation burns, among other issues. Adding to my worry, our town library director, who was in his mid-forties, had recently learned that his persistent back pain was the result of prostate cancer. His cancer had spread throughout his body long before it was ever diagnosed.

I decided to go public with the news of my diagnosis. I was surprised to find out that several men I knew in town had been dealing with prostate cancer for some time, but most of them did not want others to know they had it. One thing I had learned over the years of dealing with challenging life events was that I was not good at keeping things bottled up inside. We had benefited greatly from others who experienced similar life challenges, and I expected that grappling with prostate cancer would be no different.

Despite sharing this new challenge with others, I experienced loneliness and isolation that surpassed all of our other life experiences. It was very difficult to get through a day without drifting into a stream of "what if" thinking.

What if I discovered this cancer too late? What if I made the wrong treatment decision? Was it too late to pray for healing? Was the course of my life already determined and my fate sealed? Once this stream of thinking got started, it was difficult to stop.

Along with the thinking came a deep and abiding fear of dying before my time. My relationship with God in the face of this new discovery suddenly seemed shallow and trivial. I tried everything I knew. I read scripture. I read books about cancer, withdrew occasionally to pray at the lake where Shantel died, and sought counseling from a friend who was a pastor and also a counselor. Nothing satisfied the hunger I experienced. I was stuck in the valley of the shadow of death, and my faith was too weak to sustain me.

"God, how long have you been trying to warn me about this cancer? Is it now too late to get a cure? I have lost all faith and can't seem to get back to a feeling that you are in this with me." Every prayer I started ended with worry and fear. Patsi, on the other hand, who is normally as much of a worrier as I am, experienced an uncharacteristic peace and comfort almost from the initial diagnosis.

Up to now, through all our life challenges, I had resisted identification with Job. But just like Job, on top of all the heartache and losses that had come to my family, now my own body was under attack.

I did not want sympathy from others, but I also did not want them to trivialize what I was going through. When some learned of my diagnosis, they acted as if a death sentence had already been pronounced. That response deepened my fear. Others would say something flip like, "I've always heard that if you are going to get cancer, that's one of the best ones to have." That response made me angry. I wondered if they would feel the same way if the shoe were on their foot or if this "best cancer to have" was in their body.

On one occasion, I went to a Bristol prostate cancer support group. I was the youngest one present. The only emotion that seemed permissible among these men was anger. Many were in their seventies and eighties. I left the group that evening with a deeper sense of isolation. I never returned.

I needed to make a good decision about treatment. I also needed to get my mind around the uncertainty of my life and health. The best way I could describe it was that I needed to face my mortality. My problem was both physical and spiritual. I desperately needed God, who seemed nowhere to be found. Church services seemed meaningless; prayer time quickly deteriorated into worry, and scripture reading seemed irrelevant. A deep emptiness settled over me. There seemed to be no way out of the depression and fear I was experiencing.

I have since learned that the emotional kick in the gut I experienced is not at all uncommon for men and women diagnosed with cancer and other life-threatening diseases. We eventually come up against the realization that fears and worry rob us of our quality of life. Whether the time we have left to live is days, months or years, if we spend it in fear and worry, our quality of life has already been stolen.

91

We have to break the power that fear and worry exerts over our lives. We commonly accept that our attitude greatly impacts our immune system and natural defenses against disease. But how do we fight the tendency either to become overwhelmed by fear, or to try to deny its existence? How do we find the direction that God wants us to take when we are caught up in fear and worry?

Up to that point in my life, I confess that I had been judgmental about Bible characters who had received clear signs from God and then doubted him. I used to think that the Israelites were faithless. They had walked across the Red Sea on dry land and watched Pharaoh's army destroyed behind them, yet in less than a month, they doubted God again and complained that he had brought them out of Egypt only to starve them to death.

Peter had seen the miracles, walked on water with Jesus—and still he denied him repeatedly.

I told myself that if I had received those signs from God, I would not have any trouble trusting him completely. But here I was, having just seen God move so many people to respond to our needs, yet faced with the diagnosis of cancer, I responded with fear and worry rather than trust and assurance.

In Jesus' most important sermon he teaches us that we are blessed if we are poor in spirit. He tells us to come to him if we are weak and heavy laden. In 2 Corinthians, we learn that he answered Paul's request for healing by telling him that his power was made perfect in Paul's weakness (2 Co. 12:9).

After scouring the internet for information, speaking to everyone I knew who might have some useful information to offer, and spending countless hours worrying about the right treatment decision, I was about as poor in spirit and heavy laden as I had ever been in my life.

As I struggled and worried, a physician friend encouraged me to get a second opinion.

"If I were in your shoes, I would go to a university research hospital where they deal with this kind of cancer all the time. I would try to find a place where a team of doctors are willing to review your results and give you a definitive recommendation."

This advice made sense, but should I go to Bowman Gray in North Carolina, the University of Virginia in Charlottesville, or the VCU School of Medicine, formerly known as Medical College of Virginia, in Richmond?

One Sunday afternoon, with all of this confusion and fear swirling around in my head, a clear thought flashed through my mind.

You need to call Tim and tell him what's going on.

Tim Hodges was a lifelong friend of mine who lived in Richmond. A few minutes later, I heard the phone ring. Mark answered and brought it to me. "Who is it, son?" I asked.

"It's Tim Hodges."

LESSONS LEARNED

I share this personal struggle with fear and worry because I believe it is a common problem for many of us, even those of us who are believers in Christ. I believe that God wants to teach us about anything we rely upon other than him. Fear and worry are common indicators that we have a problem with fully trusting God in our circumstances. It takes the form of rumination and "What if" thinking that we are unable to control. In a wilderness experience, we need to be at our best to make decisions and choose the right paths going forward. Fear and worry distort our ability to see clearly and make the right choices.

Getting stuck in rumination and fear also destroys our quality of life and robs us of the joy that is in every waking living moment.

There is a rich tradition of theologians describing the "Dark Night of the Soul," beginning with St. John of the Cross, a sixteenth-century Spanish mystic. More recent books have been written by psychiatrist, Gerald May, and Thomas Moore, a psychotherapist and former monk. These men describe periods of spiritual desolation accompanied by feeling abandoned by God. It brought me great comfort to know that some of the mystics who ultimately had enjoyed the deepest relationships with God

93

had suffered through periods of time when their usual ways of relating to him, no longer brought them comfort and solace. The diagnosis of prostate cancer left me hungrier than ever for a relationship with God. Ironically, it seemed that nothing that had previously brought me comfort: prayer, worship, Bible study, etc was working for me during this period.

The good news is that God can do his best work in us when we are poor in spirit and turn to him. But we have to learn to surrender. To surrender to God when we have always relied on our own self-sufficiency is one of the most difficult lessons of the wilderness.

In the next chapter, I will help you learn how to listen attentively for God's whisper and surrender yourself to his will. Confronting fear was an extraordinarily difficult challenge for me, and it required extraordinary action to break the power certain fears had over my life.

CHAPTER 8

FINDING
THE INVINCIBLE SUMMER

What can we do when wilderness circumstances seem to separate us from God at the time we need him most? Why do the spiritual practices that used to bring comfort no longer connect us to a sense of God's presence? If we are having these doubts and fears, does it mean that we are lacking in faith, and if so, what can we do about it? How does God use these experiences to teach us to draw closer to him?

In the midst of winter, I finally found that there was within me, an invincible summer.
—Albert Camus

I shared with Tim my recent diagnosis of cancer and my dilemma about which treatment to choose. Tim said, "No wonder I had you on my mind." Later, I considered the odds of my thinking of Tim at precisely the same time that he felt led to call me. I had been praying for guidance, and this seemed to be the best lead I had received so far.

On the basis of that "coincidence" I decided to get a second opinion from the VCU School of Medicine, formerly called the Medical College of Virginia (MCV) in Richmond, where Tim lived. I called Joel Silverman, a friend and faculty chairman of the School of Psychiatry at MCV. Joel was more than willing to help me arrange a consult with a radiation oncologist and urologist. My hope was that they would review my medical file and make a specific recommendation about the best treatment for my particular clinical situation.

On the day of the consult, Patsi and I first met with a urologist. He advised me of his training and experience in the field of prostate cancer. He had done his urology fellowship at a nationally famous medical teaching facility and performed many radical prostatectomies every year. He had no hesitation whatsoever with my medical picture. He strongly recommended surgery. My spirits lifted as we waited to hear from the other physician. Patsi and I were greatly relieved.

Next, we saw a physician who was with the Department of Radiation Oncology. He advised us that my medical picture presented a clear case for radiation. He recommended that I start taking hormones to reduce the size of the tumor and then he would perform thirty-six treatments of external beam radiation.

My spirits plummeted. My anxiety, about which treatment option to choose, quickly returned. With my head spinning and my gut churning, I sat in the lobby of the hospital trying to make a decision. I made this trip to get a definitive recommendation, and now it seemed I was back to square one.

Reluctantly, I decided to leave town without choosing a course of action. I learned that if I chose removal of the prostate gland, I would need to give two pints of blood in advance of the operation, in order to have it on hand if I had significant blood loss during surgery. This was routine with prostate cancer surgery. So, I went to the Virginia Blood Services to give the first pint in case I elected the surgical option. As I got out of the car, I asked Patsi to try to contact Tim to see if we could get together before we left town. After giving the pint of blood, I returned to the car to find Tim talking to Patsi in the parking lot. "That's odd. . . ." Tim said. "I haven't been in this part of town for several months, but this afternoon I was attending a meeting just a few blocks away, and I was just finishing up when Patsi called." That struck us all as another interesting coincidence. Tim called his wife, Bev, who was leaving work, and we all went out to eat together.

After supper, I explained to Tim the spiritual longing I felt as I faced this cancer, and the hunger I was experiencing for a closer relationship with God. Tim got very excited, and without providing an explanation, he jumped up, and said, "Follow me."

"Follow you where Tim?"

"I don't have time to explain. Just follow me!"" Bev just rolled her eyes.

Tim and Bev jumped into their car and headed out to the east end of the city. Patsi and I followed them up to

Church Hill. Tim led us into a courtyard, jumped out of the car and yelled out to a person across the parking lot.

"Ben . . . Ben, I want you to meet someone. . . . Jerry this is Ben. Ben this is Jerry. Jerry needs a personal spiritual retreat here at Richmond Hill. Will you help him arrange it?" Ben shook my hand, quickly agreed to arrange a retreat if I contacted him, and went back into his meeting.

Tim took some time to explain what was involved with a personal spiritual retreat at Richmond Hill. Richmond Hill was formally a Catholic monastery. In the mid 1980s, Ben Campbell, an Episcopal priest, converted it to a retreat center for the churches in the Richmond Metro area. Silent retreats were made available, and participants could choose the guidance of a spiritual director to help them discern God's will and leadership in their life. As soon as Tim described the process, I felt an immediate and growing hunger for the experience.

A few days after returning to Marion, I thought over the encounter with Tim and Ben. I could not be sure that I was making the right decision, but I needed to move off of dead center. The idea of a retreat at Richmond Hill was strangely compelling. The more I considered it, the more I felt drawn to it. Surgery appeared to be the best chance to eradicate this cancer for a person of my age. If it failed, radiation was still available as a back-up treatment option. However, if I chose radiation and it failed, surgery was not an option. I committed myself to surgery and set a date. I also contacted Richmond Hill to arrange for a retreat when I returned to give the second pint of blood.

I arrived at Richmond Hill and made an appointment to meet with Ben after supper. Ben began with prayer and then asked me why I came. I explained all of the events my family had experienced over the previous year, and my recent diagnosis. I also shared my fear about the outcome and the deep longing I was experiencing for a more personal relationship with God.

Ben advised me to rest when I was tired, remain in silence, and to meditate upon scriptures that he would assign. He gave me the scripture of Psalms 139 to read but also said that I should not be concerned if it did not speak to me. He recommended that I follow any leading I was feeling and advised me to keep a journal. Ben prayed for God's guidance before we parted, He also reserved an appointment with me for the following day.

I wore a sign that read "Silence" and ate meals in an area that was set aside for those on silent retreats. I had no idea what to expect, but I felt good about honoring the need that I had been feeling. Ben had a gentle, authoritative presence. He impressed me as someone I could trust, someone who could help me seek God's will for my life. The accommodations were comfortable; the residents were loving and prayerful. I settled into the routine at Richmond Hill, which was to meet three times a day to pray for the city of Richmond and surrounding counties. I found out that they had been praying for me by name even before I arrived.

I slept. I read scripture. I wandered around the beautiful grounds overlooking the city. I thought about all that we had been through in the past year; my job, the boys' legal problems, the accident, my mother's death, Jamie's estrangement and surgery, the addition to the house, Mark's surgery, my diagnosis—what a year it had been!

I had many questions: Had I made the right treatment decision? Would I survive this cancer? Was God with me and guiding me? Live or die, would he give me the strength to deal with what might lie ahead? More than anything, I needed a new sense of his presence in my life.

Growing up in Tabernacle Methodist Church in Poquoson, I had experienced God's presence mostly in the way that John Wesley described his encounter at Aldersgate Street; a strange warming of the heart. Even as a child in a relatively stoic church, I felt that I was being welcomed and touched by a loving presence. When as young adults, Patsi and I sensed that God was leading us back to church, those same emotions were quite strong. It was as if heaven were rejoicing at my decision to seek a relationship with God and return to church. At that time, I strongly identified with the prodigal son returning home to the loving Father.

As the newness of this adult relationship with God wore off, I continued to identify God's presence with those emotions that would sometimes come out of nowhere when a hymn was sung or a sermon was given. Over the years I have had the same problems as most Christians discerning God's will for my life. I have experienced leadings and unusual coincidences. Sometimes a passage of scripture or a book spoke to me. But I had never sensed that God was actually speaking to me. At least not until now.

100

About eighteen hours into this retreat, I began to journal to God:

> *I believe you led me here Lord. I believe that in this pain and fear you want to comfort me and give wisdom that will carry me through whatever lies ahead. Lord, your comfort and courage are precisely for these times of fear and doubt. "Let not your heart be troubled. . . ." This is your promise to us down thru the ages.*
>
> *Lord, I know I am yours. I have grown closer to you thru each tragedy and heartache. You have never failed me, and I know you won't fail me now. Speak to me Lord . . . I am waiting upon you. My life is so short and insignificant in comparison to you, and yet you are a personal Lord.*
>
> *Lord, you are here to help us make peace with the knotted and tangled parts of our lives . . . accept what we cannot change, embrace it . . . open ourselves to all that lies ahead. Whatever the future brings, your blessings will see us through. In fact, even in the hurts and tragedies you will provide people and coincidences that will bear your blessings.*

Gradually as I wrote and sat in stillness, I sensed a presence that seemed to be responding to my questions. It was as if God had joined me and was encouraging me to ask him for answers. The words that came back to me had an authority and wisdom that melted away my fear and left me with a sense of peace and awe. This voice was not

101

audible but seemed to come into my consciousness from deep inside me. It was different from anything I had ever experienced. I decided to question and enter into dialogue with this new presence.

> *You must be Born Again.*
> *What is it to be born again?*
> *It is to step out of the world's paradigm and into mine.*
>
> *In the world's paradigm, it is not possible for one God to care for and personally tend to all that lives and moves, Christians who ask and seek, and all others who seek.*
>
> *In God's paradigm this is happening every day. God gave us his Son and his indwelling spirit. How do we know he is speaking to us? The indwelling spirit is where we join him. It is him, and it is us. When I feel touched by his spirit, it is the internal awareness that we are One.*
>
> *How do we set a course and make a decision? We try to still our thoughts, expel our doubts, slip out of the world's paradigm to whatever extent we are contaminated by it, and move into his paradigm.*
>
> *The internal place where we are one . . . and then let the dialogue begin.*
>
> *What are the questions in your heart . . . right now…today…and how would you behave differently if you knew the answers?*
>
> *God . . . do you heal? Do you intervene in our lives in a physical way to stop cancer cells from growing . . . to restore health to the diseased?*

I laid the foundation of the earth. Man under-stands much, but I know all. You know that I move people through my Spirit, which lies within them just as I move you to reach out to a person who needs to hear what you have to say. Look at the addition to your house. Consider how it came into being. Do you have any doubt that I touched others and sent them to you in your time of need?

None.

That is an example of my reality, my para-digm. You know how busy everyone is, how diffi-cult it is to squeeze even one evening out of one's schedule, let alone coordination of effort . . . team-work. And yet you have that addition. The fears you had about not having enough money or how you would coordinate it proved to be unwar-ranted.

So now consider that you have this cancer. You knew you had it. You weren't surprised at all. Stunned by the impact maybe, but not surprised.

No, not surprised at all.

In some cases, I have led you on in spite of others' doubts. Led you to Bristol, where it was confirmed that you had it, but led you on to Rich-mond to one who is especially skilled and intent upon removing it. I have led you to St. Mary's Hospital for the surgery and placed you among believers. So, even if I just move and influence people thru my Spirit, do you have any doubt

103

*that I am working in this on your behalf? See the
guideposts, retrace the road in your mind, and
become confident that I am leading you and others. Trust and obey.*

"Trust and Obey" was the hymn that my mother
requested to be sung at her funeral.

*You cannot know what the future holds. But
know that you are on course. I will be glorified in
you. I have made and will make your life a living
testament. You are special to me. I love you more,
much more than you can know. I prepared your
mother to bring you up in my way, even before
you were born. Her spirit of wonder is within you
and now is perfectly one with my spirit, as she is
perfectly one with me.*

*I have much to teach you and your children.
My word will not come back empty. Everlasting
means through you to the future. You are part of
that stream of life connected to the revelation of
old and connected to the revelation yet to be given.*

I stopped and considered what I had just written. The
stream of communication gently but firmly broke into
my consciousness. The words were uncharacteristic of my
worried state of mind at the time. The effect it had on
me was calming, assuring, understanding, and loving—so
loving. I was both excited and nervous about sharing it
with Ben.

Ben listened calmly and gave me a simple straightforward response: "It sure sounds like him to me."

As I continued with the retreat, God continued the dialogue.

I intend for you to learn my way and truth and light, my view of reality. Be prepared to shift your thinking, as you had to do when Shantel died. You had to struggle with the fact that I loved you and was present for you thru my Spirit and my Spirit in others. And yet I did not intervene to save her from death.

You must be prepared to shift your view of reality, give up what you believe and prepare yourself for what I am doing. Remember what I said through you to others. I may not give you what you want and need, but if you persist, if you stay the course and keep your eyes upon me, you will never be disappointed with the blessings I will bestow.

To be healed and whole in the spiritual sense, prepares you to handle whatever you have to face.

Lord, what then should I do to prepare for the blessings you have in store for me in this experience?

Stay hungry and thirsty for me, and I will feed you. Let go of your own understanding and seek mine. Remember to feed on me in your heart and lean not on your own understanding.

Devote the time as you have recently, as you are doing today. Give me a day of your undivided attention. Ask what you will and then listen.

Expect that this experience will lead you into a deeper relationship with me—simply because you are needy now. In one sense, you are needier than you ever have been, because it is your life that hangs in the balance. Embrace this neediness. Don't run from it or try to avoid it. Open yourself to it and I will use it to teach you.

Teach me what, Lord?

Teach you not to waste time in a frivolous way, as if you will live forever. You will not. Teach you to make this day count for something in my kingdom. Teach you even deeper compassion for those who suffer, who struggle.

106

God went on to give me specific guidance for the relationships with each member of my family. He advised me to be supportive of my companions at work, but to divest myself of the negative emotions they shared with me.

As I reread and meditated on the experience, I clearly understood that the words had come through my thoughts—but they were definitely not **from** me. The wisdom was remarkable and spoke to my needs at the time. The experience transcended the needs in my life and continues to guide me.

I am still amazed at the flood of difficulties that came upon my family in less than a year's time. But I am even more amazed at how God met us at every turn with encouraging friends, love and guidance. He drew me hungry and thirsty to Richmond Hill, where he waited for me to get quiet enough to hear him. And I began to understand what he was teaching us. It was an old, old story of his light shining in darkness, his strength overcoming my weakness, his blessings flowing out of our suffering. He was revealing a deep, timeless wisdom that is woven throughout scripture and demonstrated in the life of Jesus.

Several weeks later, I underwent surgery at St Mary's Hospital. Tim and Bev prayed with Patsi in the waiting room during my operation. I experienced absolutely no fear or worry about the surgery or the treatment decisions I had made. The surgeon expressed confidence that he had been successful in removing all of the cancer. The pathology report confirmed that we had clean, cancer-free tissue around the removed gland.

I recovered quickly. Follow-up lab work detected no measure of PSA, which confirmed that the surgery had been successful. But I remembered that God had not promised a cure of the cancer. What he said was that I was on the right course and he was healing me in the spiritual sense. As hopeful as I was that the cancer was gone, I wondered why God had not told me I would be cured.

Two years later, my PSA started rising again. It was an indication that the cancer had escaped the prostate gland before surgery. My battle with this disease was just beginning.

LESSONS LEARNED
I believe that the experience at Richmond Hill was one that God specifically designed for me. Early on in my diagnosis, the coincidences involving Tim caused me to

107

suspect that God was going to use him in the spiritual healing God wanted to send into my life. As soon as I knew that such an opportunity was available, God gave me a deep hunger for it.

What can we learn from this experience that applies to all of us who are lost in a disturbing wilderness experience?

God uses circumstances of our deepest need and greatest vulnerability to teach us to transition from self-reliance to greater dependence upon him. When we come to the end of all we know to do and turn to him in faith, he will find new ways to speak to our heart and direct us through the wilderness.

An encounter with the Living God drives out all fear and anxiety. It opens us up to the flow of grace and mercy that is truly indescribable. It transcends our systems of survival and self-reliance and leaves us with a deep trust and peace. When we are in his will we will experience that peace that passes all understanding.

But the way God wants to speak to us may be quite different from the ways he has spoken to us in the past. In fact, the ways we have experienced his presence in the past may seem particularly ineffective. So, we need to seek and stay open to new and different alternatives. He has a way of stirring up a hunger for the way he wants to speak in our current situation. So, we need to be attentive to the "coincidences" that he sends into our lives to get our attention. It could be a book he wants us to read or re-read, a person who offers suggestions we are not expecting, or recurring messages that are pointing us to an experience we would not otherwise choose.

The sooner we get away from blaming ourselves and God and the sooner we can take a position of trust with hope and expectation, the sooner he will be able to send us the signs that point our way through the wilderness.

God is waiting for us to get quiet and still and earnestly seek him with all of our heart. Finding and protecting sacred places in our lives where we can take uninterrupted time to be alone with God are important for continued growth in the faith. We have only to look to Jesus and his example to see how necessary it is to draw away from the noise and confusion of our age (Matthew 14:23; Luke 5:16). I will discuss in Chapter Twelve one of the ways (Centering/Contemplative Prayer) that has been particularly helpful to me.

CHAPTER
9

YOU CAN COME HOME AGAIN?

There is no easy pathway through the wilderness of a loved one with addiction. How do we find our way through the gut wrenching and confusing experience of a loved one who has fallen into this disease? How do we love them without enabling their addiction; confront them without driving them away from us?

. . . Father, I have sinned against heaven and against you. I am no longer worthy to be called your son.
—Luke 15:21

We admitted we were powerless over alcohol—that our lives had become unmanageable.
—Step 1 of the 12 Steps of Alcoholics Anonymous from *Twelve Steps and Twelve Traditions*[2]

My heart was breaking for our son, Mark, as I prayed during the Christmas Eve Service at our church.

---

2 *Twelve Steps and Twelve Traditions* (New York, NY: Alcoholics Anonymous World Services, 2004), 5.

*God, can't you do something? We have begged
and pleaded with him to stop drinking but it's
getting worse. Now he has two DUI's with more
certainly on the way, if he doesn't kill himself or
someone else first. God, tell me what to do, what
to say to stop him. Now he's on the verge of losing
another job.*

The tragedies of Shantel's death and Matthew's injury
struck the family quickly. The damage was done before
either event reached our awareness. But Mark's tragedy
was unfolding in slow motion before our very eyes and
well within the reach of our love and influence over his
life, and yet we were still powerless to stop it.

We were desperate to get through to Mark. How
could he fail to see God's grace in our lives and continue
to destroy himself with drugs and alcohol? In desperation,
I began writing a letter to the family that year to remind
them of all we had overcome, with God's help. I called it
The Blessing. On Christmas Day, I wrote these words to
Mark.

*For you, son, I feel the greatest need this year
to write and speak of my love for you and God's
love for you. I know there have been times this
past year that, except for the grace of God, you
could have destroyed your life or someone else's—
permanently. As I sat in the Christmas Eve Service last evening, I begged God for there to be a
break in your destructive habits so that the Bless-*

112

*ing that he has for you and the love that we have
for you can get through.*

*This phase of your life is temporary, Mark.
Winston Churchill once said, "When you are going
through Hell, don't stop!" So, I say to you this
Christmas Day—Don't stop. Keep going through
this phase and out to the other side. Decide to be
the wonderful person that lies within you. Decide
to stop setting yourself up and sabotaging your
happiness.*

*Let's spend time together this year, just you
and me. Let's work together to break away from
the past. I want to help you so badly, and when
you decide, you will find a fulfilling life without
alcohol.*

113

It had become increasingly clear over the previous
three or four years, that Mark had a serious problem with
alcohol and drugs even though he was still in his early
twenties. It was clear to us that he was in a downward spiral. He had separated himself from our church and all his
friends who were moving in a positive direction.

Dating back to middle school, Mark had gotten in
trouble every year, almost like clockwork. As soon as he
lived down one problem, he would set himself up all over
again. We could easily trace some of the causes. He had
struggled academically and was placed in special education classes after being diagnosed in elementary school
with dyslexia, and ADHD. When we broached the subject of college, he swore that he would never put himself back into the pain and anxiety that he experienced

struggling with schoolwork. He chose instead to become a carpenter and work in construction. We supported his decision although we always sensed that he compared himself unfavorably with his brothers.

Matthew had his own problems with substance abuse. But Matthew absorbed schoolwork like a sponge, and he was also gifted athletically. After graduating from high school, despite his spinal cord injury, Matthew completed two years of community college while holding down two part-time jobs. He transferred to Christopher Newport University in Newport News, and appeared to be leaning toward a career in rehabilitation counseling. Mark's older brother, Jamie, also had problems with drugs and alcohol, but he managed to avoid legal problems.

114

Mark's problems with alcohol were qualitatively more serious than those of his brothers. Mark was completely unable to control his drinking. After taking one drink, he continued until he blacked out. When he woke up, he stubbornly refused all offers to drive him home. He demonstrated real potential in the jobs he took in carpentry, but he could not get up in the morning after staying out all night, and his employers eventually gave up and fired him.

The family gradually came to realize that Mark was an alcoholic. Even Mark knew he needed to break free from the habits and relationships he had fallen into in Marion, so he agreed to move with us to Richmond when I took a new position as Assistant Commissioner. But Mark brought his problems with him. Soon after the move, we found him passed out on the steps of our apartment. Later, when we bought a house in Mechanicsville, Mark picked up two DUI's in two years, continuing his annual pattern of self-destruction.

Once he completed the required driving classes and counseling imposed on him by the court, he decided to leave Richmond and move to Newport News where Matthew was attending college. After about a year living with Matthew they determined that they could not live together in harmony, and Mark decided to get his own apartment.

Patsi and I became more and more preoccupied with Mark's deteriorating situation. Like most families watching a loved one struggling with substance abuse, we were conflicted about what we had done and should be doing to try to stop Mark from destroying his life. We knew the next conviction would be a felony, which would result in major lifelong consequences: the loss of his driver's license and the loss of his right to hunt and own a firearm, one of his favorite pastimes. Without a driver's license it would be difficult if not impossible to practice his carpentry trade. If he did not get caught, we were convinced that he would continue to drive drunk and eventually lose his life or kill someone else. After Shantel's death and Matthew's spinal cord injury, we knew better than most that we had no immunity from yet another tragedy.

We knew Mark suffered from poor self-esteem, which had been evident since his middle school years. But we feared he would never recover from the guilt of manslaughter and felony prison time. The irony of it all was that both Patsi and I began our professional careers as substance abuse counselors. I spent my entire life working with those who suffered from disabilities and emotional problems. But now we could only helplessly watch our own son take the same destructive path of people we had counseled over the years.

So, we worried and prayed and worried more. We asked everyone we knew to pray for him; our friends, our Sunday school class, our family. We tried to maintain contact with Mark, whenever he would allow us, to make sure he knew how much we loved him. I often pulled him aside to plead with him to stop drinking before it was too late. I even tried, unsuccessfully, to get him to voluntarily put an ignition lock breathalyzer system on his vehicle to keep him from drinking and driving. Every day, we worried and tried to come up with a solution to stop this slow-motion train wreck.

Patsi and I struggled and sometimes argued about what to do. Maybe we should toughen up on him and do a family intervention. Something along the lines of: *We love you Mark, but until you come to terms with your drinking, we are not going to visit you anymore or invite you to family gatherings.*

It made sense from a treatment perspective, but it never felt like the right thing to do.

Our hearts sank when Mark called us from the Newport News City Jail in March. He was now charged with his third DUI. If convicted, this one would change his life forever. The questions flooded in again. Have we been too accepting of his behavior? Should we have cut him off from the family? And what should we do now that he is locked up again?

Yes, You Can Come Home Again.

These questions swirled in my head, as I took my lunch break to attend the Lenten services at St Paul's Episcopal Church in downtown Richmond. I came to worship that day sad and broken-hearted. All of our efforts had failed. What should we to do now? Should we draw the line between Mark and the family until he stopped drinking? I cried out to God to break into our circumstances.

His answer to my prayers came that day, spoken **117** through the visiting pastor, Lance Watson. God was about to surprise us with circumstances we could not have imagined, and Pastor Watson's sermon provided the foreshadowing of miraculous events to come. Lance, a gifted speaker and leader of St. Paul's Baptist Church in Richmond, took his message from the three parables that Jesus used in Luke: The lost sheep, the lost coin and the lost son—the prodigal son. The title of his sermon was **You Can Come Home Again.** He spoke of the love of our heavenly father who never gives up on us and waits for us to have a change of heart and turn back home. He refuted those who have said throughout the ages that you cannot go home again. He reminded us that God is concerned with separation and longs for us to come to our senses and cry out to him. He spoke from that scripture in Luke that marked the turning point in the life of the prodigal son.

When he came to his senses, he said, "How many of my father's hired servants have food to spare, and here I am starving to death! I will set out and go back to my father and say to him: 'Father I have sinned against heaven and against you. I am no longer worthy to be called your son; make me like one of your hired servants.'" So he got up and went to his father. (Luke 15:17–20)

I walked into the service that day confused and broken. But I left with hope that this would be the turning point in Mark's life that would lead him to open himself to the help he so desperately needed. Lance's sermon convinced me that my job was simply to pattern my love for Mark after the love of the Heavenly Father, who endures the pain of waiting for us, all of us, to turn back to him. I left with a hopeful prayer that circumstances would somehow bring Mark back home to us where we could try again to share our love for him.

When we visited Mark in jail, we saw the first hint that this jail-time might be having a different effect on him. He said to me through the thick glass that separated us in the visiting room:

"We are Deans. We will get through this, won't we Dad?"

I responded, "Yes. We are Deans. We have overcome many hardships in the life of our family. And we will get through this one, with God's help, **if** you will admit that you have a problem and commit yourself to getting the help you need."

118

One week after his arrest, he was released on $10,000 bond on the condition that he would get himself into treatment and live at home with his parents until his trial. Lance Watson's message from God echoed in my spirit. **Yes, you can come home again.** This was the beginning of a series of miraculous events that would reveal to us that God was right in the middle of our circumstances and guiding us through this new wilderness experience. A modern-day prodigal son story was about to unfold.

When our Sunday school class learned of the events, a friend gave us the name of a person who had helped their son get clean. We called John Shinholser with the McShin Foundation, the day before Mark's release. John said that timing was critical and that we should bring Mark in to see him at 8:30 the next morning. We learned that John was a former active duty marine sergeant with over twenty years of sobriety.

After a brief discussion, John suggested that we leave Mark with him. He would enter Mark into a day treatment program. Mark would shadow John, as he worked with addicts and alcoholics in recovery and needing recovery. In the evenings, he would return home to live with us. When we left Mark that day, he hugged us, and with tears in his eyes he said, "This feels right. I think it's going to be OK."

That afternoon when I picked him up, he was sitting in a group with other "newcomers" listening to others who had from several weeks to several years of sobriety. One that I will never forget was Virginia, a short black woman who was overflowing with wisdom and hope. She spoke a simple message: "If I can do this, then you can too."

She had given up a crack cocaine habit and a life of destruction. Now she owned her own home, drove her own car and worked a job at Walmart. It was clear to me in just a few minutes that Virginia's real job was to spread faith, hope and tough love to anyone who would listen.

Over the year that followed, John took Mark with him wherever he went, to jails, hospitals, NA meetings, recovery houses, and court hearings. Mark got a firsthand look at where his disease would take him if he failed to follow through.

120   Mark opened himself to John's help and the support of those recovering in Richmond. He attended multiple Narcotics Anonymous and Alcoholics Anonymous meetings every day. Even though alcohol was the primary drug that he abused, he identified more with the younger men who were involved with NA. He attended campouts and social events and completely immersed himself in the powerful, contagious, recovering community in Richmond. We were amazed at his openness and honesty. Many evenings after he returned from John's program, Mark would share the insight he was gaining into his individual disease as well as how he had used our family dynamics to support his habit. We realized that we needed to change with him.

The one thing that haunted Mark the most was the looming court trial. He was ready to face the consequences. Each time his court date would come up, his trial would be postponed. Mark's frustration increased with each cancellation but Patsi assured him that God has a way of working all things together for good even when we don't understand. Mark had our assurances that God was working on his behalf, but he longed for a clear undeniable sign that God was on his side. And God provided that sign on the day he appeared before the judge, ten months after his arrest.

We were advised that the Commonwealth Attorney wanted to meet with us before Mark's court appearance. We joined her in a room just outside the courtroom, and she said,

> I am about to do something that I hardly ever do, and I really don't know why I am doing it. I have more than enough evidence to convict you of your third offense in less than five years. If the judge asks me why I am doing this I cannot give him a good answer. You are clearly guilty of a felony, and you know that a felony would ruin your life, don't you? All I know is that every time I have reviewed your file I have gotten a nudge to give you a break. I don't know . . . maybe it's from God. I don't know if you believe in God or not, but you should know that you are blessed. Most people who come before this court do not have the support that you have here with you today. Do you know how blessed you are? If you screw this up, it will not only come back on you, but it will also come back on me and your attorney. We are all going out on a limb for you. If you blow this opportunity, I can assure you that you will never get another break like this one.

121

Mark was allowed to plead guilty to a second offense. He was sentenced to six months in jail with all but thirty days suspended. He lost his license for ten years but was allowed to request a restricted permit in three years. Most importantly, he avoided the felony conviction. He was permitted to get his affairs in order before returning to serve the balance of thirty days in jail.

After the court adjourned, the Commonwealth Attorney waited for me and Patsi outside the courtroom. She hugged both of us and asked us if Mark knew how blessed he was. We assured her that he did. She wished us well. This was clearly not the typical encounter with the person prosecuting your son.

Mark's response to this was, "You could have knocked me over with a feather. All this time I wondered if God was in this with me, and all the time, he was working in the heart of the person whose job it was to prosecute me."

As unusual as it was that a Commonwealth Attorney would risk saying what she said to us, the rest of the story is even more remarkable. After Mark served the remainder of thirty days in jail, Patsi and our friend, Shirley, drove to Newport News at midnight to bring Mark home. Our Sunday school class placed a banner across the back door of our house for Mark to see when he arrived that read "Welcome Home, Mark."

Later that day, I attended the Lenten Service at St Paul's Episcopal Church, exactly eleven months to the day from Mark's arrest. God spoke this time through Reverend James Lemler from New York. You might have already guessed that his sermon was from Luke 15, titled, "The Lost Son and the Extravagant Love of our Heavenly Father."

I was overcome with emotion, and my tears flowed throughout Reverend Lemler's message of reconciliation and forgiveness. I could not resist standing aside after the sermon to share with him the part he had played in our story. He responded, "What a blessing to be a part of such a wonderful story of God's amazing grace!"

Later that evening, family and friends gathered to celebrate Mark's return and successful completion of his jail sentence together with eleven months of sobriety.

"We had to celebrate this happy day, for your brother (and our son) was dead and has come back to life! He was lost but now he is found!" (Luke 15:32, NLT).

God has provided remarkable answers to prayer in our family's lifetime, but none as extraordinary as this.

Mark maintains his sobriety many years later. He managed to stay employed during one of the worst economic recessions in recent history. He earned a respectable living in the remodeling business, despite the fact that he had no driver's license for three years. He now works as a superintendent at a respected construction firm in Richmond.

Mark has been an inspiration to many others. He has confronted his illness with honesty and courage. We have been amazed with his deep wisdom as jobs have dried up and he has pressed forward to the next opportunity. More evenings than not, you will find him in a Twelve Step

Meeting. He would rather take a beating than to speak publicly, but he regularly shares his life experience with those in need.

LESSONS LEARNED

Our circumstances were quite unique, and the answers to prayer were unusual and extraordinary. While each family's circumstances are different, there are elements of our story that are applicable to all families who are struggling with this disease. Patsi and I had both worked with substance abuse in our professional careers. The following wilderness lessons are universal, and I hope you will find them useful as you travel this very difficult journey with your loved one.

124

A person with substance abuse must reach rock-bottom before coming to look for an alternative. Each time that person cycles through a painful experience, such as arrest or incarceration, it presents an opportunity for recovery.

Whatever pain we are protecting people from experiencing denies them of the opportunity to reach their bottom. So, we must carefully think through our tendencies to get them out of jail quickly, hire attorneys, and otherwise protect them from the painful consequences that their behavior is producing in their lives. This is so much easier said than done. It is very important to educate yourself about how you might be enabling a loved one's behavior. This requires considerable introspection, and help can be found in the company of other families who have already spent time on this journey. Though we may try to fix them and the situations they create, all we can really do is learn how we are reinforcing their behavior and then stop enabling. Families Anonymous and Al-Anon are good places to start.

While our tendency is to keep our loved one's addiction a secret, resources are available. Corporate prayer is a powerful weapon in combating addiction. God cannot use others to lead us to those resources if we get caught up in the shame and guilt of this disease and keep it a secret. We found that we needed to carefully choose from the help that was offered, as was the case when we were dealing with the loss of our daughter. But we are convinced that God is leading and guiding in all wilderness experiences, and he has a way of connecting us with those whose help we need.

The letting go and the never-ending love of the father in the story of the Prodigal Son are wonderful examples to all of us. In our painful wilderness journeys, we have to permit our loved ones to exercise their God-given capacity for free will. Nothing we can do can force our loved ones to come to terms with their disease. This fact creates considerable frustration for those of us who care deeply for them. At the same time, we should never give up hope. Each consequence has the potential to bring them to their senses. The loving father in the parable of the Prodigal Son did not run after the son when he left home. He did not protect him from the painful consequences of his behavior. But he waited hopefully and expectantly for a sign that his son was ready to change his behavior and come home. And then he rushed out to embrace him and welcome him back into the family. Somehow, he had managed to hold onto his hope and love for his son despite the justification he had to write him off. Praying for that patience, hope and love is so important in these situations.

125

PART III

BEING TRANSFORMED BY THE WILDERNESS

What does God want to teach us, and how is he using the wilderness to reshape our life stories? How does God want to use our experiences in his master plan?

RECONCILIATION, RECOVERY, AND HOPE

What are some of the models that teach us how to find our way through the emotional wilderness experiences of our lives? How can we use the experience of being poor in spirit as a gateway to finding our way to hope and recovery? How does unforgiveness block our pathway to healing? What preconceptions, behaviors and beliefs do we have to give up in order to clear the way for God to do his will in our lives? What are the things we can do to activate our God-given guidance system through a wilderness experience?

We suffer to get well. We surrender to win. We die to live. We give it away to keep it.
—Richard Rohr

Mark's story illustrates the extraordinary lengths God will go to in order to heal our hurts and hang-ups and to draw us back to his love. Henry Freeman's story is another.

In Chapter 3, I shared part of Henry's story of the tragic death of his daughter and granddaughter. Carla and Jenny were killed instantly when they were run off the road in Wytheville, Virginia, by a truck driver who fell asleep at the wheel. Henry, who is Caucasian, attended our grief support group but continued to struggle with forgiveness for the African American truck driver. His anger and hatred spilled over to all truck drivers and all African Americans. Cindy, Henry's surviving daughter, watched her dad cling to this seething resentment. She tried in vain to get him to forgive, but his hatred took on a life of its own, threatening his health and blocking his healing.

130

Some years later Cindy developed a chronic intestinal problem that required her to be transferred to the VCU Medical Center in Richmond. The day of her operation, Cindy shared her family's loss and her prayers for her father with an African American hospital worker who transported her to surgery. This worker had grown up immersed in the gang culture of Richmond, but now she was actively involved in her church. Cindy asked her to take care of her parents, who were in the waiting room together with two pastors from Marion.

The hospital worker went to the waiting room that day and did her best to cheer up the crowd. As she joked with them about her past life, she demonstrated her strength by picking up Henry's pastor from behind in a big bear hug. That sent the group into uproarious laughter, mixed with just a little nervousness.

She shared Henry's story with a friend from her church, and several days later, on her day off, the two of them came back to the hospital to visit Cindy and her parents. After checking on Cindy, they turned to Henry and said the following: "Cindy told us about the death of Carla and Jenny by a black truck driver and how this has caused you to hate people of our race. You may be unaccustomed to this, and it might be uncomfortable for you, but if you will let us, we would like to do something for you now."

Henry was embarrassed and reluctant, but he nodded his agreement.

They brought out a bowl, filled it with warm water and dropped to their knees in front of him. Henry sat in stunned silence as they gently removed his shoes and socks and washed his feet.

131

Henry says that as they performed this act of love, his tears began to flow. God's love, expressed through these two women, cleansed his heart. Years of resentment and hatred simply melted away and never returned. God designed this extraordinary act of love and humility to release Henry from the unforgiveness that interfered with his healing.

Blessed Are the Poor in Spirit

Our life experiences convince me that God waits patiently for us to turn to him, particularly when we are desperate and broken hearted. Jesus reminded us of this when he said that the poor in spirit are blessed. I used to wonder why this particular promise was in the Sermon on the

Mount. How can it be that we are blessed when we are poor in spirit? Poor in spirit is what we feel when we don't know where to turn. It's the experience that comes when we have lost someone very dear to us, or when life, as we have known it, has been turned upside down by some traumatic event, illness or disease. It is the place where we recognize we are hopelessly addicted to drugs or alcohol, or, after much denial, we finally recognize that we have a physical disability or mental illness that we will have to contend with the rest of our life.

Throughout my career, I have worked in the helping profession with those struggling with substance addiction, mental illness, and intellectual disabilities. As a believer undergoing difficult life experiences, I searched for understanding in the Bible and the behavioral sciences. I have read many books dealing with the human condition and the spiritual journey.

When our family was devastated by a loss, followed by injury, and then illness, I did what we all do; I tried to escape those places of pain and suffering, tried to think positively, tried to use my will to bend my circumstances and my emotional responses back into shape. I have always held demanding jobs, and I told myself I could not afford to dwell in the depths of despair. But the feelings and the consequences of serious life difficulties don't bend to our will, no matter how hard we try. Pain is part of our lives, and suffering comes to all of us if we live long enough. So, what is God's will for us as we hit these inevitable periods in our lives---when we are poor in spirit?

132

Step One in the Twelve Steps of Alcoholics Anonymous is "**to admit that we are powerless over alcohol, that our lives have become unmanageable.**" It continues: "**We perceive that only through utter defeat are we able to take our first steps toward liberation and strength.**"

I have come to believe that this step of admitting that our lives are out of control, and unmanageable is an essential part of healing, no matter what difficult life experience we are dealing with. In our western culture of independence and self-determination, being poor in spirit is difficult terrain for us to occupy. Our initial reaction is to struggle frantically to get in control and return to our previous sense of normalcy.

Things would be ok **if only:** I had taken better care of myself, my daughter was still with me, I could have said and done the right thing to keep my husband from leaving and so on. But reality, as we have previously understood it, does not exist for us any longer.

These events strip us of our egos, our sense of control, and our sense of who we are. They reveal our vulnerability. Our identities must now undergo radical change. This is very disturbing for us since we have spent our whole lives trying to build up our identities and ways to protect ourselves. So, it is not unusual that we would resist this kind of ego demolition.

Christians are not immune to this process. Most of us start out with the belief that if we behave ourselves and go to church, God will protect us from harm. This small and

133

misguided understanding of God must be jettisoned, as we move forward into reconciliation and recovery.

It is only after we begin to give up on our attempts to return to the way things used to be, that God can begin to work to bring about healing. When we stop running the **what if** scenarios in our head, stop blaming ourselves or someone else for what happened, and come to realize that life is what it is, the work of reconciliation can begin. We may experience a deep emptiness for the first time. Once we come to these painful realizations, we are entering the life position of being poor in spirit.

And God has been waiting for us to get to this place. It is here that we realize how much we need him, maybe for the first time in our lives.

134

Amy Grant has a song that beautifully describes God's response to us when we finally realize how much we need him. It thrills my heart every time I hear it. The song is entitled "Better than a Hallelujah." In it she says that God has a special place in his heart for those of us who are suffering and turn to him in our despair. He hears the cries of drunkards, the dying, and soldiers praying for their lives. And he hears us better when we are at the end of our ropes than when we are on top of the world and singing out with our shouts of Hallelujah. We are so reluctant to go into these dark wilderness places in our lives, and yet God is waiting for us there, hoping and longing for us to turn to him.

When we give up and cry out to him with our broken hearts, we are entering the position of being poor in spirit.

And we have to fully embrace this reality, let it teach us, allow our self-reliance to be stripped away, let our need for God seep into our hearts and minds. Marcel Proust writes, "We are healed of a suffering only by experiencing it to the full."

I believe that if we experience our suffering to the full without hope, without God, we risk dying "the second death," described by Jerry Sittser in his book, **A Grace Disguised**. The loss of our loved one, health, job, or relationship is the first death but it is not the worse kind of death. The most tragic loss is the second death—the death of the spirit, which comes when we choose to continue to live in despair, hatred, or bitterness. The first death happens to us; the second death happens in us. It is the loss of hope. It is living in the land of the poor in spirit, the wilderness valley of the shadow of death, without God. This is the death from which Henry was saved, by the women who confronted his resentment by lovingly washing his feet. It is the death from which we all need to be saved.

Holding on to Hope and Watchfully Waiting on the Lord
Step Two of the Twelve Steps is: "We came to believe that a power higher than ourselves could lead us to sanity." This is an action statement of hope and a display of one's trust in God.

Once we have fully embraced our suffering, refused to run away from being poor in spirit; once we have stopped chasing the false genie god that is at our beck and call, our next step is to open ourselves to the true God.

135

C. S. Lewis once wrote, "**I want God—not my idea of God.**" So, we learn to die to what we were and who we thought God was and enter into the mystery of who God is and what he will now do in our lives, to save us from the second death of our spirit. This is a process of looking to God with a sense of expectation. Even though it involves surrender and waiting, it is an active process. Here we learn to hold the pain of suffering while we wait for God to reveal himself to us.

Learning to surrender and wait on God is not easy. It takes a daily discipline. Otherwise we turn it over to him, start worrying, and take it back. To give it to God means to acknowledge that we are not in control. It's not up to us. But we are not just waiting, and, by surrendering, we are by no means giving up. On the contrary, like a tree or plant that has gone many days without rain, we learn to send our roots deeper, where the living water flows. We are watchfully waiting for the Lord to renew our strength.

As we watchfully waited on God during our periods of suffering, he led us to people and ideas that provided us with a road map to healing. When help comes from God, it fills an empty place in us and moves us forward on our journey towards healing. I have found it helpful to keep a journal especially during the most difficult seasons of life. When we document our prayer requests and surrender them to God, it is more difficult for us to attribute the answers that come to mere coincidence.

The idea of a road map is a powerful concept. The speaker in a tape I listened to after Shantel's death, presented the idea that there is within each of us, a God-given road map to healing. These roadmaps are unique and individual, and they remain dormant until activated by a loss. Just as we have an immune system that helps us fight off infections and illness, we have a psychological and spiritual system to lead us to healing in times of trouble. That concept brought me enormous comfort and started my search for the signs of God's leading.

Years later, I met an author and speaker, Dr. Al Siebert, who reinforced this idea. Al spent much of his career researching the concept of **resilience.** His message is that we can learn to discover and enhance these healing systems that are part of each of us. We can go beyond surviving and learn to thrive in the face of difficulties. In order to activate our road map, our system of resilience that leads us through the valleys of our lives, we have to choose hope and refuse to die the second death.

137

Reconciling Our Losses

Our grief support group had been meeting for about a year after Shantel's death, when Mal Brown, Jr., the director of a local funeral home, was perceptive enough to host a workshop featuring Dr. Alan Wolfelt. Alan is one of the nation's most compassionate and knowledgeable grief experts. Alan spoke personally to those of us suffering great loss and invited us to share our hurts and questions about the experience of grieving.

He introduced us to the concept of **reconciliation,** a different way of thinking about our losses. He taught us that the life that none of us would ever choose has come upon us, and now we must learn to integrate this new reality into our lives. We gradually realize that we will not **get over** this loss. We come to understand that we cannot insulate ourselves from the pain. We have to contend with a new normal.

Reconciliation is a process in which we begin to fully accept the reality of our situation and decide that it will not destroy us. We come to expect and accept the strong bursts of feelings that ambush us without warning. We begin to anticipate and plan for holidays, birthdays, and anniversaries that remind us of our losses. We begin to accept that death is final in this world, and that our loved one is not coming back. We learn to integrate our grief and suffering into our personality and allow it to change our identity. We begin to focus less upon what is missing and more upon what we have left in our lives.

Reconciling a loss is to internalize the message that Patsi and I have learned from many different sources over many years: You will survive this if you choose to. It will not be easy. It takes years, not months. Your roadmap through the wilderness is unique but you can learn from others who have been forced to take the same journeys. You will never get over this completely. But if you choose to, you can learn to re-form your life around it. It will impact every aspect of your life, your body, your mind and your spirit. Your faith will be put to the test but you will grow stronger. Normal for you now has a new definition. It includes a lot of things that you previously considered abnormal. You will have good days and bad days. Sometimes you will feel like you

138

have fallen back into the pits of the wilderness. But you have a choice. You can choose to live in the sadness of this experience for the rest of your life, or you can search for others to help you crawl out. If others can survive this, then you can do it too.

Reconciliation means finding new meaning and purpose. For Patsi and me, that purpose came to us from our children. We considered that even though we had lost one child, we were still blessed with four living children that needed our love. We recognized that we had to choose life—ours and theirs. We began to understand that if we allowed the grief to swallow us, we would lose them, and each other too.

Another purpose emerged more subtly over a longer period of time. As warden and director of the mental health institute, I felt it was my duty to attend funerals of employees and their families. Patsi and I began to notice a change in the way others going through loss received us. We now felt their pain at a much deeper level. They could tell from our tears, that attending their loved one's funeral was painful for us, and they expressed gratitude for our sacrifice. When someone in the community lost a child, we had a special bond with them. When we shared our tears and hugs, we discovered that doing so had a powerful effect. The cards we sent and visits we made carried a love and authority that was beyond us. This bond and influence provided us with a foreshadowing of how God intended to use our loss to help others.

The Power of Recovery

Another powerful idea that has helped us and countless others to manage a loss or disability is the concept of recovery. We are experiencing recovery when we take a negative disabling condition or life event and transform it into a positive thing that not only dramatically improves our lives but also releases our potential to help many others. Recovery has been around for many years in the treatment of addictions. More recently, the same idea has been used to understand and manage mental illness.

Bill Wilson began to describe the concept of recovery in 1953 in his book, *Twelve Steps and Twelve Traditions.* He recognized alcoholism as a spiritual problem that required a spiritual solution. He described the need for a power greater than ourselves that he referred to as the **higher power**. Step One is to admit that we are powerless over alcohol and that our lives have become unmanageable. Step Two is to come to believe that a power greater than ourselves can restore us to sanity. Step Three is to make a decision to turn our will and our lives over to the care of God as we understand him.

Thomas Keating in his book, *Divine Therapy and Addiction*, and Richard Rohr in *Breathing Underwater* expand the applicability of the Twelve Steps **to all of us.** They explain that those who do not have an addiction do have compulsive patterns of thinking, feeling, and behaving that we falsely believe will gratify our needs. The human condition is such that we all struggle to achieve happiness, security, affection, and control in ways that cannot be successful except through a complete dependence on God. Reaching a point where we recognize our need to have God in our life is where the journey of spiritual transformation begins. The more aware we are of our need, the more likely we are to surrender ourselves to the only true source of peace and joy. "**Blessed are the poor in spirit.**"

The way I have come to understand what Bill Wilson, Richard Rohr and Thomas Keating are saying is that we are all suffering from a disability or disease whether we call it addiction or the human condition. We grow up operating under the illusion that we are able to achieve happiness and protect ourselves from harm through our own efforts. Those of us who have encountered addictions, disabilities, or other traumatic life events, have the opportunity to learn how unmanageable our lives become. As our illusions are shattered and our egos stripped, we have the option to fill the void with an increasing intimacy with God. The task is not for us to reestablish our coping mechanisms, but to learn to live in an increasingly dependent and surrendered relationship.

In my case, I believed that if I lived my life preparing for the worst-case scenario, I would be able to stay in control, protect my family from harm and myself from failure. I attributed my success to my ability to anticipate problems before they happened and to be ready well in advance, just like my father taught me to prepare for hurricanes when I was a child. The peace and joy that God had for me was buried deep under all my anxious antic-

141

ipation and preparation. Achievements that should have brought joy such as my education, promotions, awards, and so forth, were short-lived. I had to quickly return my attention to the threats I supposed were still just ahead.

The tragedies that visited my family initially justified my view of the world as a dangerous, unpredictable place that required me to redouble my effort. Eventually I faced the fact that I could have never anticipated or adequately prepared for any of these events. More importantly, in each case the support, love, and grace that saved us was from a source that I could not control. Ultimately, I had to conclude at ever-deeper levels that I was powerless over my life. God continued to offer me the option to trust him and turn control of my life over to him. The major sustaining power in my life was operating, **not because of**, but **in spite of** all my frantic effort.

Recovery is an idea that has God's fingerprint all over it. Every once in a while, humankind stumbles upon a reality that has been woven into the fabric of the universe from the beginning of time. Recovery is one of those truths. Early in Mark's recovery, I attended a Twelve-Step meeting with him at St. Mary's Hospital. That particular evening the discussion was on Step Two, the Higher Power. People around the circle shared their beliefs about the nature of their Higher Power. In that group of about thirty people, I doubt that there were more than a handful who attended church on a regular basis. There were those who professed to be Christians, Jews, Muslims, and some who were doubtful and unbelieving. As I listened to

142

the speakers describe their Higher Power, a wonderfully loving and forgiving image of God emerged. Listening to these addicts and alcoholics describe God warmed my heart and brought tears to my eyes. In all of my years in church I have not heard a clearer and more convincing description of the loving Father.

Why does recovery work? I think it works because it starts by helping us admit the true unmanageability of our lives. It helps us to strip away the illusion that we are in control and that bad things don't happen to good people. It works because it turns us to God, the only true source of peace and joy. Recovery works because it taps into the legitimacy of one person with a negative life experience showing another how they can change their life. Recovery is underway when our hope springs forth and our internal system of resiliency is activated. With the love of a Higher Power forgiving our past mistakes, we can begin the process of honest self-examination and exploration of our future.

It was nothing short of a miracle for Mark to face his dependence upon alcohol and drugs at age 25. But the biggest challenges he has overcome are the little frustrations that have occurred on a daily basis. The deer that decided to cross the interstate directly in front of him that almost totaled his truck, the jobs that have dried up unexpectedly, the employers and coworkers that have relapsed, making a living in the construction industry with no driver's license, having the DMV overrule the court to extend the suspension of his license.

143

Patsi and I have worried that these frustrations would result in his relapse. But Mark has faithfully attended meetings and pressed on. From time to time, he shares with us just a bit of the wisdom that he has absorbed from the Twelve-Step community. When frustrations have occurred, he has said, "Well it's life on life's terms." Or when we voice our fear about the long-term consequences of his conviction, he tells us, "I know, but I cannot dwell on that. I need to focus on one day at a time." When someone deals dishonestly with him he says, "I just need to do the next right thing." And with that profound straightforward wisdom, the support of his friends and his faith, he has persevered.

When I have joined him at Twelve-Step meetings and events, I have sensed that I am an adopted member of a large and loving extended family. I once asked Mark, "What saves you from relapsing?" He responded, "I have learned that I cannot control most of the things that happen to me. I also cannot control the feelings that follow and the desire to use again. But I don't have to **act** upon those feelings. I am in charge of how I respond."

Choose Hope

Recovery could not exist as a life-changing reality without hope. Hope is the essential spark that is passed from a recovering person to one who is poor in spirit. Hope keeps us from dying the second death. When we encounter a tragedy, loss, disability, or addiction, and we fully admit that we need God, he will send help. If we seek, we will find hope among those who have survived and been transformed by their losses, those who can say with full authority: "If I can do this, you can do it too."

Hope activates our roadmaps and our inner system of healing and resiliency. When we pass it on to others, we become partners with God and part of his master plan. This gives meaning to our suffering and helps it count for something much bigger than ourselves.

But what if I don't feel hopeful? What if all that I experience is despair, depression, and hopelessness? This is the critical stage where our free will is essential. As Mark explained, we cannot control what happens to us, and our feelings of despair and hopelessness follow close behind. What we do control is how we respond. Feelings come and go and are generally unreliable.

There is a story of "The Eagle and the Wolf," which makes this point.

> There is a great battle that rages inside me.
>
> One side is the soaring eagle. Everything the eagle stands for is good and true and beautiful, and it soars above the clouds. Even though it dips down into the valleys, it lays its eggs on the mountaintops.
>
> The other side of me is the howling wolf. And that raging, howling wolf represents the worst that's in me. He eats upon my downfalls and justifies himself by his presence in the pack.
>
> Who wins this great battle?
>
> The one I feed.

We choose what part of our personality we feed. We choose whether or not we use a hardship to justify a neg-

145

ative lifestyle. Whenever we fall down, we have a choice to stay down or get up again. God will not violate our free will to snatch us from a mental hole we are digging for ourselves.

I don't want to oversimplify this essential part of recovery and reconciliation. Sometimes there are long periods of time when we do not experience God's presence and action in our lives. Walking through the wilderness is no picnic. Sometimes we are hurting so bad we can't feel God. Sometimes God withdraws the sense of his presence for a time. But nothing has changed. He is still walking with us and teaching us to move from baby food faith to mature spiritual food while we wait with trust and expectation.

146

In my experience, God expects us to make a choice about our allegiance. Whether the circumstances require us to stand firm or step out on faith, God always requires initiative and choice on our part. In the end, it is not our act nor our prayer that changes God. We are simply setting the stage for his hope to choose us.

LESSONS LEARNED

This entire chapter consists of lessons we learned in dealing with the difficult experiences we have encountered. But here are some of the lessons that I think are worthy of summarizing and repeating as you search for your individual pathway through the wilderness.

There is a great blessing in coming to grips with being poor in spirit. If we can fully embrace that life position without losing our faith and hope in God we can learn to surrender to his leadership. This is not easy but if we look to scripture and to the methods that work for those who struggle with the most difficult wilderness experiences, we will find evidence that they have been inspired by God.

God's blueprint for recovery is imbedded in the Sermon on the Mount as well as Paul's recognition that God's strength and power is perfected only in our weakness (2 Corinthians 12:9). The Twelve Step movement brilliantly puts these principles into practice. All of us have our addictions and attachments; those things we trust and depend upon other than God. The principals have much to offer all of us who seek a transformed relationship with God.

Hope is the spark of encouragement that there is a way through the wilderness and that God is with us providing leadership and guidance. Sometimes hope is difficult to find, and if we are trying to find our way alone it is very elusive.

The best place to find hope and encouragement for healing is among those who have survived the wilderness and are choosing to give to others what was given to them. In these groups, we will find those who are learning to survive along with others who have transformed their experience. God includes these people in our lives, but it requires personal transparency and sharing. In this age of the internet, many of us try to work this out on our own rather than sharing our deep need with those we know.

Learning to embrace our human condition while at the same time exercising our free will choice is one of the most valuable lessons of the wilderness. We always have choices when it comes to how we handle a tragedy in our lives. Being poor in spirit does not mean that we are powerless. It simply means that we are depending upon God for the resources we need.

CHAPTER 11

THE THIRD SIEGE

What should we do when we seem to be under attack by random and unconnected circumstances? What is our most direct pathway to deepen our relationship and reliance upon God? What are the individual survival strategies that we need to surrender to God? How can God possibly use our life disturbances to reform and transform our lives for his purpose?

Consider it pure joy my brothers and sisters,
whenever you face trials of many kinds, because you know that the
testing of your faith produces perseverance.
Let perseverance finish its work so that you may be mature and
complete, not lacking anything.
—James 1:2–4

If we truly believe these opening lines from the book of James, we would be rejoicing when trials and hardships break into our lives. But most of us, even if we are among those who earnestly long for God's will in our lives, are seeking peace and happiness instead. It is our nature to avoid pain and suffering, to pray for the times of testing to pass us by and if they come, to be short in duration. Sure, we all like a little challenge in our lives and most of us understand that we are strengthened when we are tested, but we would rather select those periods on our schedule and for the duration we choose. But life doesn't come at us that way. When trials come, they often arrive when we are least prepared. They come clumped together like a series of waves striking the beach. One wave knocks us down and as we are struggling to get up, three more crash in on us.

What do we do when the tests come? How do we protect ourselves and fight back when we come under attack? One thing is clear from our life experiences: whether we like it or not, trials and tragedy will eventually come to all of us if we live long enough. If you are not experiencing one right now or emerging from one, then look out. And perhaps the most important question is: How does God use these tests to grow us and transform us to do his Kingdom work?

The Third Siege

There have been three periods in the life of my family when I felt that we were under attack from unseen forces intent on our destruction. The first period followed Shantel's death, when we also lost Brittany, our first grandchild, and Jorja, my brother's wife. The second was eleven years later, when the twins were injured, my mother died, and I was diagnosed with prostate cancer. Then there were the years in our lives that I have come to consider "the third siege." It was a time when every member of our family came under attack. A time when God taught me about fear. Not just fear in the general sense, but the fear and hunger for control I had carried all my life—the fear that kept me from trusting him and him alone. And he taught me about prayer.

The first crisis of that period began when Mark was arrested for his third DUI. He had been trying to stop drinking and even managed to get through the New Year's celebrations without alcohol. But in March, he went to a bar where he continued drinking until he blacked out. Two police officers were in the parking lot outside the bar, when Mark got behind the wheel of his truck. He jumped the curb making it crystal-clear that he was in no condition to drive himself home. He was arrested and locked up in the Newport News City Jail, one of the toughest places in the state to be incarcerated. Different from his other incarcerations, he was not released the next morning. He had to wait a week to appear before a judge, and he was required to post $10,000 bond. This time, the authorities were serious.

There were little irritations during that period that started innocuously and grew in significance over time.

Jamie, our oldest son, married Johnna the previous year while he was still in nursing school and she was studying to become a dental hygienist. They both graduated in the spring of that year and decided to move to Richmond. They settled into a beautiful apartment in Henrico County. Unfortunately, the person who lived just above them was, to say the least, difficult. She made her complaints known to them by stomping on the floor whenever they made the slightest bit of noise. Jamie loves music and plays several instruments, so this was particularly annoying to him. As time went on, Jamie and Johnna tried to adjust their lifestyle to avoid complaints. However, the neighbor became increasingly sensitive to any sound they made. The situation worsened over time, and eventually she went over the heads of the apartment management and filed repeated complaints with the police. Jamie and Johnna tried to stay calm and collected throughout the ordeal, but after several months they knew they needed to get away.

They planned a dream vacation. They had both achieved scuba certification, so they arranged a diving trip to Curacao in the Caribbean, one of the best diving locations in the world.

After their first day at the resort, a thief on the beach stole all their cash, credit cards, and identification. Jamie spent the remainder of the week trying to replace his cards and making arrangements to get back home. Without identification, they missed a connection flight, which forced an overnight layover in Aruba. With only a small amount of cash, not enough for a taxi and hotel and no credit cards, they were forced to leave the tiny airport when it closed for the evening.

A security guard they **hoped** was benevolent arranged for them to stay with his parents in the country. As they traveled along bumpy back roads to an uncertain location, Johnna admits that she had never been so afraid in all of her life. All she could do was cry and think of Natalee

Holloway, the cheerleader from Alabama who had disappeared in Aruba the previous year. Their dream vacation had become a living nightmare. The guard's parents welcomed them with open arms, and though there was a language barrier, Jamie said he could easily tell that they meant them no harm. The language of love and good will is universal. The guard returned them to the airport the next morning, in time to catch their flight home.

Some things that started out as blessings, turned sour.

Matthew graduated from college and received a full scholarship to the master's program for rehabilitation counseling at Virginia Commonwealth University. He proposed to Ashlee, a young woman he had been dating in Newport News. They moved to Richmond to take new jobs and plan for their future together. During the year, Matthew was invited to play wheelchair basketball with the Richmond Rim Riders, an organized team that competed nationally. He began to participate in regular practices and travel with the team on weekends. It was clear that he had a gift for this sport, but the combination of a full-time job, full-time school, and a new sport, threatened his relationship with Ashlee. Stress mounted, and something had to give. The closer they got to the wedding date, the more tentative the relationship became.

The assault on the family that year also involved serious life-threatening crises.

Our oldest daughter Tiffany's husband, Dwayne, developed flu-like symptoms while on a work-related trip to Seattle. After nine days, his deteriorating health forced him to cut his trip short and return home. Tiff picked him

153

up at the airport in Norfolk, and she could immediately see how ill he had become. Dwayne was exhausted from the trip and desperately wanted to go home and go to sleep, but Tiff insisted on taking him to the emergency room. Shortly after arriving in the ER, he was admitted to the intensive care unit (ICU) with a high fever. He was also incoherent, and his whole body shook violently. After many tests and consultations with numerous doctors, an infectious disease specialist was called in. Doctors eventually diagnosed Dwayne with a rare disease called ehrlichiosis, caused by a tick bite. They treated Dwayne for several weeks with massive doses of the strongest antibiotics available. Eventually his condition slowly began to improve. The medical team made it clear that if Tiff had not gotten Dwayne into the hospital when she did, he would have undoubtedly died from this disease.

154

Almost as soon as Dwayne began to improve, Tiffany faced her own health crisis. For years she had been dealing with a serious case of ulcerative colitis, which first appeared when she was pregnant with our second grandson, Nicholas. Her physicians recommended a complex surgical procedure that involved removing her colon and reconstruction of her digestive system. Tiff, fearing the possible complication of a permanent colostomy, put off the surgery for almost ten years.

Her physician finally drew the line. He advised her that her disease would eventually develop into cancer, and he would not continue to treat her unless she agreed to the surgery. After much deliberation, Tiff decided to undergo surgery. She carefully selected a doctor to perform the procedure. We checked and double-checked his credentials. He was known to be an excellent surgeon with a great bedside manner. The surgery went well.

After a brief period of hopeful recovery, consistent with her worst fears, she developed a serious abscess. The complications resulted in her being hospitalized repeatedly. Over the course of the year that followed, none of us can count the number of times that she was in and out of the hospital. To top it all off, in the middle of these complications she learned that her carefully chosen surgeon was moving out of state to take a teaching position. So, Tiffany's follow-up treatment was passed on to other doctors in the practice. Patsi traveled back and forth from Richmond to Tidewater to support Tiffany and her family. Repeated hospitalizations failed to accomplish any medical improvement. The only thing that became increasingly clear was that Tiff's physical strength and her will to live were being gradually eroded.

155

Standing by while our children experienced these hardships was difficult enough but before the year was over my own health became part of our growing list of worries.

My PSA had begun to rise again, two years after my surgery. This rise after surgical removal of the prostate gland confirmed that the cancer had escaped the gland before it was taken out. I had one other chance for a cure of the disease. So, three years after surgery I was referred to MCV for salvage radiation treatment under the assumption that the cancer was still in the prostate bed area. Thirty-eight radiation treatments did not slow the rising PSA, but it did produce the worst case of radiation proctitis that my doctor had ever seen. A surgical bypass was performed to allow my damaged bowel to heal, and we began to face the fact that the chance for a cure was over. Since treatment for cancer was now a permanent part of my life, I began looking for a medical oncologist to guide my treatment.

Eventually, I chose a doctor in Charlottesville. Consistent with his advice I began to make all of the nutritional and lifestyle adjustments to slow the inevitable growth of the cancer.

When my PSA approached 3, my doctor decided to begin hormone treatment. Before he started the shots however, he wanted to see if we could determine where the cancer might be hiding out in my body. He referred me to University Hospital in Cleveland, Ohio, for a scan designed to locate the cancer. The test came back negative, but a CT scan, which was done at the same time, showed a number of nodules in my lungs. Finding this reference in the report, I questioned my oncologist, but he was not alarmed. He explained that prostate cancer rarely spreads to the lungs and that there were many other plausible explanations for lung nodules. He did think I should get a biopsy of the nodules to rule out the possibility that they were prostate cancer. Later that fall, I was hospitalized for a biopsy. The results confirmed that the nodules were in fact, metastatic prostate cancer.

And, as if on cue, my job took on stressful complications. The position I now held was Assistant Commissioner of Facilities. While I was still Director at Southwest

Virginia Mental Health Institute, the new Commissioner, Jim Reinhard, who was a psychiatrist and a former hospital director, asked me to consider the position of Assistant Commissioner. This position reported directly to him and was responsible for the fifteen institutions for the mentally ill and developmentally disabled. After I accepted the position, an additional facility for sexually violent predators was added to the mix. In the facility system, there were over eight thousand employees with an annual budget exceeding five hundred million dollars. It was a job that overwhelmed my coping strategies on the best days. But this particular year brought even more challenges: staff conflicts that defied resolution, the need to eliminate mandatory overtime, and a goal of making all of our facilities smoke-free. The Department of Justice inspected and became particularly dissatisfied with one of our facilities. They wrote up a long deficiency report. On top of all of this, my right-hand person began to experience persistent symptoms that were eventually diagnosed as pancreatic cancer. And I was not responding well to these challenges, together with what was happening to my family at the time. My boss had to counsel me for allowing my stress to spill over onto my coworkers.

As that period ended, and we began to absorb all that had come against us I remember saying to Mark that it had become pretty clear that our enemy, Satan, was trying to spook us. It was the only way I could make sense of this string of calamities. It had become a period of fear: fear that shook our confidence in the medical establishment; fear of thieves, individuals, and insects that meant

157

to harm us in spite of our best efforts; fear that our character defects would win out over our love; and my personal fear that the attack would continue and I would not meet the test.

I knew that God was with us and had his hand on our lives. There was no way I could deny the clear evidence of his guidance through the years. But what were we to do with all of this? How did he want us to respond? What did he want me and the family to learn from these new challenges? I wanted to learn any lessons he had for me quickly and get back to the work at hand. As it turns out, God was waiting for me to ask these questions. But there were no quick fixes. God wanted me to confront a lifetime pattern of survival and self-reliance and learn to put my trust completely in him.

One thing was certain. All of the events that unfolded in our life during that period produced in me a hunger for a deeper relationship with God. I was once again teachable, ready to listen and learn.

LESSONS LEARNED

This third siege took me back into the wilderness where I became needy and teachable once again. I think that God allows circumstances to come into our lives until we learn to get it right and take the power out of the forces and survival strategies that have control over our lives. In some respects, my experience has been a bit like the movie Groundhog Day, where Bill Murray's character repeats a segment of his life over and over again—until he gets it right. Once we know that wilderness experiences are not punishment and that a loving God longs to lead us through our trials, we can concentrate on prayer and learning to surrender to him at ever-deeper levels. What follows are some things that I believe apply to all of us.

It is useful to know that we will never get a satisfactory answer to "Why." However, if we choose to rely on God and pray asking, "What is my next right step, Lord?" and "What do you want to teach me now?" he will lead us through difficult circumstances. Each successive wilderness experience teaches us new things about how to deepen our trust in God. However, some of the lessons we learn are of the Groundhog Day variety. That is, they teach us once again that we all have a basic survival strategy that we need to surrender to God at ever-deeper levels. The chapter that follows is specifically designed to help you think about what your strategy is and how you can learn to surrender it to God.

CHAPTER
12

PRAY WITHOUT CEASING

What is the difference between fear that is a healthy response to threatening circumstances and fear that indicates a lack of trust in God? What can we do to deepen our trust in God once we discover that fear and anxiety or other personal survival strategies are interfering with our reliance on God? How does God want to replace our strategies with ever increasing trust in him? How does God use our prayer to help us find concrete solutions to our needs and reveal the areas of our lives we need to allow him to heal?

Don't worry about anything; instead pray about everything. Tell God what you need and thank him for all he has done.
—Philippians 4:6 (NLT)

We did a lot of "the next right things" during that period, a concept that Mark shared with us from the Twelve-Step meetings he attended regularly. We asked everyone we knew to pray for us. This required us to be open to those around us and specific about the help we needed.

Our Sunday school class at Cool Spring Baptist Church provided a caring group of friends to pray for us. One direct answer to prayer came when one of our close friends from the class provided us with the name of John Shinholser, leader of the McShin Foundation. John connected Mark to the "contagious" recovering community in Richmond for people struggling with addictions.

Friends in Marion at First United Methodist Church regularly lifted our needs to God. Patsi's relatives in Alabama took our needs to the altar, as they had done so many times when we lost Shantel and the twins were injured. I had joined a Centering Prayer Group at Richmond Hill four years earlier. Each Tuesday evening, after our silent prayer, I would update the group with our needs, and together we would lift them to the Father.

162

Once again, most people just shook their heads and wondered how all this could be happening to one family. But once again, by asking and receiving from many loving people, we found ourselves at the center of hundreds of prayer requests.

Another right thing I did during that period was to ask Ben Campbell, Director of Richmond Hill, to provide me with spiritual direction. Ben helped me to stop trying to analyze myself and encouraged me to bring our needs shamelessly and honestly to God; to understand that all people of faith have these fears. He helped me to stop condemning my faithlessness and start searching for what God wanted to teach me.

I arranged for a personal retreat at Richmond Hill to draw closer to God and listen for his voice. On the first day of the retreat, I attended a healing prayer session. The prayer leaders lit candles and played relaxing background music to set the stage for the session. One of the leaders, Fontaine Williamson, instructed us to write our requests for healing on a card. I asked for the healing of the metastases in my lungs and healing for my coworker, Rosemarie. As I lifted my needs to God, a thought came to me: **What took you so long, Jerry?** (to come to this retreat and this healing prayer session) **You know you don't get any points for starving yourself.** God has a great sense of humor.

During the session, the leaders moved in behind each of us. They gently placed hands upon our shoulders and silently lifted our prayer requests. At the end of the session, Fontaine told me that as she lifted me in prayer, she had a vision of me at a coat check room. She saw me hand over a soiled coat to God. He returned it to me clean and pure.

As the retreat continued, I met with Janie Walker and Karen Moore, two members of the Richmond Hill staff. The more we all talked and prayed, the clearer it became that the lesson God was bringing to me, had to do with my lifelong reliance on the false gods of control and survival. During the retreat, I was led to an issue of *Weavings* in the library. *Weavings* is a Christian journal designed to promote growth and explore how God's providence and human lives are being woven together in the world. It was as if this particular issue "jumped off the shelf" and beckoned me to read it. This particular volume of *Weavings* was entitled "Security." The acting editor quoted Jesus

163

in Luke 17:33 (NRSV), where he tells his followers that, "Those who try to make their life secure will lose it, but those who lose their life will keep it."

But how was I supposed to lose my life, particularly with my strong inclination to try to control situations and prepare for all possible threats?

An article by Robert C. Morris entitled "Paradoxical Security: Trusting God in Fearful Times" examined the positive and negative sides of fear and spoke directly to my question:

> Fear itself is a divine gift, meant as an alarm to awaken the capacities of the soul that can respond to the crisis. But if we are ruled by fear, it can become the chief entry point for the dark and demonic powers to penetrate our souls.
>
> Fear not only awakens our dark side; it can shake up our faith. Even the dogmatism it can inspire is often the very sign of threatened faith—a shaky substitute for trust in the biblical sense: heartfelt confidence in God.

Despite all the evidence I had to the contrary, I was still missing that trust, that heartfelt confidence in God. Morris continued:

> I say, "shake up" faith because faith in lesser gods can masquerade as faith in the ultimate God. The blessing hidden in the dangers of the Test is that our souls can be shaken free of their attachment to the lesser gods we have confused with the true and life-giving One. Jesus, tested in the wilderness, realizes and renounces his own inclinations to become the kind of Messiah the Fear Monger would delight in.

164

So, was this was the blessing God wanted to bestow in the tests that had come to our family? Maybe he wanted to strip away my belief that I could somehow control my life. Maybe he wanted to shake me loose from my faith in lesser gods and place my trust in him. We clearly had many justifications for the worry and anxiety we experienced that year. But it was becoming clear that God wanted to teach me a different strategy for handling my fear. He wanted me to understand that my fear was not an early warning sign for trouble ahead. I was allowing fear to rule my life and providing Satan with an entry point into my soul.

Near the end of the retreat I had a memory of the bell tower of the church I grew up in. The memory was from a difficult time in my life and the life of our congregation. Factions had formed around whether to keep the pastor or have him replaced. Also, during this time in my life, I clearly saw the defects in my father. I confronted him about his anger and the way he treated us, but he never accepted responsibility for his behavior. This was when I decided that God was powerless, and I needed to take charge of my life. So rather than hold fast to my religious teaching to trust God, I used the hypocrisy that was playing out in my church and family to justify my use of alcohol, tobacco, and pornography.

The bell tower had been a scary, foreboding place when we were children, but I rebelliously decided to use it as a hideaway to smoke, drink, and look at magazines. Now at the end of this retreat, God was bringing this

shameful memory and the fear I felt back to my awareness, so that I could ask for his forgiveness and healing.
God also wanted me to forgive my father and see him in a
different light—the light of God's grace.

The Panic Room or the Kingdom of God?

In the year that followed, I continued to journal, pray,
and meet with Ben. I came to call the place of survival
that I operated from much of the time, "the panic room."
When I was in the panic room, I functioned as an atheist.
I was alone in a world of scarcity and not in touch with
God's action in my life. I saw the big picture pessimisti-
cally, and I minimized God's blessings and grace. I simply
did not trust him. As a result, I spent most of my time,
whether asleep or awake, anticipating and preparing for
the problems that might come that day or the next. Since
I had such clear evidence of God's faithfulness in my life, I
also felt a lot of shame and guilt. This condemnation was
exactly what the Enemy wanted me to feel.

But there was an alternative that was mine for the
asking. God had been teaching me that his kingdom, the
kingdom of God that Christ spoke of, was available to
me in each moment of every day. It was a Kingdom that
exists in a kind of parallel universe. But in order to step
over into his reality of abundance and blessing, I have to
renounce my faith in lesser gods. Every day in this parallel
universe, he waits for me to join him in the stillness and
listen for his guidance. Here in the Kingdom, I do not
have to struggle for survival. He provides the time and the

resources I need. Each day, to occupy this space he has for me in his kingdom I have to activate my faith, stay out of the panic room, and choose whom I will serve, the gods of Satan the fear monger, or the One, True, Living God.

The practice of Centering/Contemplative Prayer has become a daily discipline in my life. This meditative prayer that has been part of the church for centuries involves opening ourselves to God in silence and stillness. It is a prayer that beckons to us from the scripture in Psalms, "Be still and know that I am God" and from the Gospel of John, where Jesus tells us we must, "Abide in me as I abide in the father."

This prayer of silence and surrender involves setting aside daily periods of uninterrupted quiet time, usually twenty minutes and choosing a sacred word or phrase as a symbol of our intention to be present with God. When our mind starts to wander or worry, we gently come back to the sacred word. In the scriptures, we often see Jesus withdraw from the crowds to pray and reconnect with his Father. He instructs that when we pray, "go away by yourself, shut the door behind you and pray to your Father secretly. Then your Father who knows all secrets will reward you." (Matthew 6:6, NLT)

This method of prayer gives God access to our old hurts and woundedness. Over time, he heals us from the inside out. The contemplative prayer of stillness and surrender somehow gives him access to our unconscious. The sacred phrase I used during that period was "Your Will, Your Way Lord."

Exercising my faith and staying out of the panic room were like strengthening a weak muscle. Some days it worked, and other days I fell back into the old patterns. But God continued to teach me about my fear and my faith.

I have made it my goal to spend more and more time in the parallel kingdom. When fear rises, I know he wants me to run to him as a first resort instead of to the panic room. I still have a "little atheist" that is part of my spiritual makeup, but it's getting weaker and less influential in my daily life.

The Rest of the Story

I have read many books and scripture about prayer, but I still don't understand how it works. What I do know is that God wants us to pray shamelessly and honestly, and he wants us to ask others to pray for us. By doing this, we have to admit to ourselves that we are not in charge of our lives; he is.

God taught me that year that I did not have to struggle to find the right words to pray to him. He was already in those situations, long before the needs ever came into my awareness. And he would be there long after I moved on to something else. So rather than my finding the right words to call his attention to the needs of those situations, he instead was calling me.

Lessons Learned

It was a period of deep need. I knew I needed to get in a teachable position once again. God had taught me many lessons about fear and self-survival, but the lesson was not over. He allowed another wilderness experience to reinforce my need to reject my false gods and fully rely on him.

All of us have those false gods; those strategies we rely upon other than the true and living God. We have the scriptural reference of Jesus being driven into the wilderness by the Holy Spirit after his baptism. God stood back and allowed Satan to take his best shot at his son. But even though these periods are unpleasant and difficult for us, something constructive is happening, something powerful that is within the new definition of power that Jesus gives us . . . the power that is perfected only in our weakness. Figuring out our personal temptations and their antidotes frees us up to be open to God's call on our life.

169

We can never underestimate the power of corporate prayer. God already knows our needs and is already working in ways we sometimes cannot understand to bring about his love and good will in our lives. However, praying and asking for prayer is essential because it helps us to realize our need for God and moves us into right relationship with his will. It also connects us to helpful resources he wants to bring into our lives.

Learning to surrender to God on a daily basis is the most effective antidote for fear and anxiety or any other survival strategy we have taken on. Centering prayer, practiced regularly, is one way to learn how to surrender our lives to God moment by moment, learn to trust him ever more deeply, and allow him to heal us from the inside out.

God is seeking to bring our past hurts and sins into our awareness, not to condemn us but to have us lay them before him and find alternative ways to live in trust with him. Living in the kingdom of God is not just a promise for the afterlife. God gives us an opportunity to step into the flow of his abundant mercy and grace, every day. Finding a way to surrender daily is critical not only when we are in wilderness experiences but also when circumstances return to normal. As we deepen our trust and relationship with God, he reveals how he wants to transform and use us in his kingdom work.

CHAPTER
13

GREATER THAN
OUR SUFFERING

If God makes all things work together for good,
does he cause us to suffer to bring about his will in our
lives? Is a relationship with God an insurance policy
against bad things happening in our lives? What kind
of story is God trying to write with our lives? How does
he want to use our wilderness experiences to accomplish his kingdom work?

The most authentic thing about us is our capacity to create,
to overcome, to endure, to transform, to love and to be greater
than our suffering
—Ben Okri

Most of us know of Paul's promise in Romans 8:28,
that God works all things together for good for
those who love him and are called according to his purpose. It is not only an observation from Paul, but a thread
of hope that runs throughout the Bible. It begins in Gen-
esis (50:20), when Joseph tells his brothers, "You meant it

for evil, but God meant it for good" (author paraphrase). So, the promise is clear. God wants to help us transform our suffering to accomplish the work of his kingdom. But how does this play out in our lives? Some take from this and other similar verses that God is the author of pain as well as love. In this way of thinking, God causes all things to happen so that he can fulfill his plan in our lives. People express this by saying, "This must be part of God's plan, and I/you just need to accept it." This explanation works for some, but for some of us, it proves to be problematic. When we encounter a tragedy like the loss of a child, we must come to terms with God's nature and how he works in the world.

Many of us start out believing that if we are children of God, we somehow have an insurance policy against suffering and hardship. My answer to these issues comes from the book of Job, thought to be one of the oldest books in the Bible. In the opening chapter, God stands aside to allow Satan to strip Job of his health, wealth, and loved ones. In the end, after much speculation by Job's friends as to what God is up to and what Job did to deserve such punishment, God arrives to speak for himself but refuses to offer an explanation. Job responds by giving up his questions and choosing to accept God on God's terms. God does not cause Job's losses, nor does he protect Job from the devastation that Satan delivers.

I don't believe for a minute that an all-loving God took our child, paralyzed our son, caused another to be addicted, and planted cancer in my body to achieve his purposes. What I know is that he has worked in all those situations to protect us from evil, help us survive, and hold onto hope. He has also helped us use these experiences to assist and encourage others. We have somehow become part of his plan to bring healing out of heartache. And our wilderness experiences have somehow transformed us to be used by God.

The Bible offers no explanation for why God allowed Satan to take his best shot at Jesus in the wilderness, immediately after his baptism. But it is clearly written in Matthew, Mark, and Luke that the Holy Spirit led or drove Jesus there. So, Jesus' wilderness experience was part of God's plan and clearly not punishment for his sins, as Christ was sinless. And the temptation came from Satan. After his experience in the wilderness, Jesus not only survived the physical and spiritual temptation, but he emerged with clarity and strength that propelled him all the way to the cross and beyond. Immediately following his wilderness experience, Jesus initiated his ministry, selected his disciples, began healing the sick, and preached the greatest sermon of all time that begins with, "Blessed are the poor in spirit." And thereafter, Jesus often withdrew from the crowds to return to the wilderness to pray and commune with his heavenly Father.

173

What can we know about God's story and his plan for humankind? If we exercise the free will he has given us and choose to seek him in all situations, how does he protect us from evil, even while he allows harm to enter into our lives. How does he use us and our wilderness experiences to advance his master plan? How can the most tragic events of our lives become our most important developmental milestones?

John Eldredge, best-selling author, tackles these questions in a little book entitled *Epic: The Story God Is Telling and the Role That Is Yours to Play*. In the Prologue, he quotes J. R. R. Tolkien from *The Lord of the Rings*, when Sam turns to Frodo and says, "I wonder what sort of tale we've fallen into?"

Eldredge explains that Sam could not have asked a more important question at that point in their journey. Such a question amid the beauty, events, and danger that had befallen them implied that there is a larger story being played out, and they have somehow tumbled into it.

Eldredge suggests that the question, "What sort of tale have I fallen into?" is an important question for all of us to ask, maybe the most important of our lives. This little book is one that grabbed my attention while Patsi and I were on vacation on Hilton Head Island. For a number of years, I had experienced a leading to write to my family to help my children and grandchildren see how the events of our lives so clearly testify to God's love and point us to the roles we are to play in his plan. This little book prompted me to begin compiling the stories of our family, for our family, in a writing I entitled **The Blessing**. It is my answer to Eldredge's question.

The stories I have shared in this book testify to the extraordinary ways God has intervened in the life of our family—not to shelter us from loss and tragedy, but to assure us of his unfailing love as we have survived the valley experiences. But surviving the losses has only been part of the story. Cooperating with God, as he has worked all things together for good, is the rest of the story—the

174

story that continues to unfold in our lives. We are not unique. The mystery and power of using suffering and tragedy to help others plays out in thousands of support groups and Twelve-Step meetings that gather daily all over the world. I am convinced that recovery and transformation—our capacity to overcome, endure, and be greater than our suffering—are all part of God's master plan.

And if we are to become partners with God in his triumphant parade through history, we must let his message of hope pass through us to others. When we do, we become part of his kingdom. We get in on the deal, the really big deal. We become a small part of a very Big Thing. There is no work more important than this.

Let me illustrate with one final story. When I came to Richmond to take the position of Assistant Commissioner, Patsi and I started searching for the church that God wanted us to join. We knew from experience that tragedy can strike in the blink of an eye. We also knew of the importance of being connected to a praying, supportive church family. We attended several different churches throughout Richmond and Ashland but received no clear leading from God. We were looking for a contemporary worship service and a place where our experiences could be used to help others.

Cool Spring Baptist Church was less than a mile from the new house we purchased, so we decided to give it a try. We loved the contemporary worship service, and quickly found a Sunday school class that allowed for open discussion and sharing. But there were a number of obstacles that caused me, in particular, some hesitancy. One of the first was that they did not recognize my infant baptism in the Methodist church as a valid baptism. If I wanted to join Cool Spring Baptist, I would have to be baptized by immersion. Patsi had been immersed as a young woman, so she was good to go. My spiritual ego rebelled against the idea that my infant baptism was somehow insufficient.

I wondered if there would be other theological issues that I would find inconsistent with the traditions I had come to accept.

There was also no clear leading at Cool Spring Baptist as to how our past experiences could be used to help others. We met with several of the staff and shared our life experiences. At First United Methodist Church in Marion, we had organized a congregational care ministry. Our volunteers were trained to reach out to members experiencing sickness and all kinds of losses. But the staff at Cool Spring seemed to have this care ministry well covered, and offered no strong indication of needing our experiences or my "splendid" organizational skills. So, my spiritual ego got no boost here, either. However, since the job I had taken on as Assistant Commissioner was so consuming, and since I had very little energy left over at the end of the day, I decided to wait and see what might emerge as time went on.

Larry Frakes, the longtime pastor of Cool Spring, lived in our new neighborhood and helped me to set aside my hesitations. He explained that each Baptist church is autonomous, free and independent to make local decisions. Cool Spring had decided to maintain the connection to the Southern Baptist Convention in large part because of their strong emphasis on worldwide missions. These explanations helped us to move toward membership at Cool Spring.

Most importantly, we felt that God wanted us in this particular church. When my ego would wrestle with the pros and cons of joining the church, God would whisper, *This is not between you and them, Jerry; it's between you and me.* The message was consistent, and as time went on it gradually became clear to us that this was where he wanted us. So, it appeared that I needed to set aside my spiritual pride and be obedient to his call, even though I could not see how it fit into his plan.

In the end, I decided that if baptism meant that I loved the Lord, then I would be glad to be dunked every day. I was learning to scuba dive at the time, and I joked with Larry that I was going to bring some of my gear to the ceremony. With Larry's encouragement, I arrived for my baptism with my face mask and snorkel in hand. Larry held it up for the entire congregation to see and said, "You see this? Some people just don't trust me."

We joined the church in February. In August of that year, Doug Grote, the recreation pastor at Cool Spring, left his three-year-old daughter, Kristen, in the vehicle in the church parking lot. She suffocated. Doug had just returned from a mission trip overseas and was dealing with jet lag as well as the many distractions of catching up on his job. Dianna, Doug's wife, came to Doug's office in the afternoon, and together they went to the daycare center expecting to take Kristen home. They were told by the workers that Doug had not dropped Kristen off that morning so they thought Kristen was with Dianna. Minutes later, when her lifeless body was found in the back of their car, Doug's painful screams echoed throughout the church.

Patsi told me about this tragedy as I returned from work and was heading out to mow our lawn. God spoke to me over the drone of the lawn mower. *This is why I called you to this church, Jerry. It's time for you and Patsi to give back what was given to you. Start a grief support group.*

The entire church was devastated by this loss. Three-year-old Kristen had gladdened the hearts of all who met her. She attended daycare at the church and the whole family, Doug, Dianna, Kristen, and their son, Dayton, were an important part of the church family. Counselors were brought in to help people in the congregation deal with this tragedy.

The entire Richmond Metro area wrestled with this event. The news media was relentless in its coverage of the story. Doug was charged with a felony and became the subject of radio talk shows and newspaper editorials. The righteous indignation was palpable. How could he forget about his daughter? Why shouldn't he be prosecuted to the fullest extent of the law? How could a loving parent do such a thing? How could anyone who had done this ever again be an effective minister?

Patsi and I spoke with Marsha and Darrell Rettig, who were part of our Sunday school class, about starting a support group. They lost their daughter, Jenny, in a car accident a few years earlier. They agreed that we should do whatever we could to help with the intense suffering

178

that had engulfed our church. I approached the church leadership about starting a group and received unanimous approval. The church, and our pastor Larry, surrounded Doug and Dianna with love beyond measure, and whole-heartedly supported Doug throughout the legal proceedings. The church family's loving response to Doug became a defining moment in the history of the Cool Spring congregation.

Our group continues to meet, and God has used it to touch many hurting people. It is often hard to tell who is the most blessed by this group, those of us who lead it or those who come for support. One thing has become clear as we have shared our losses and joined with others in their suffering. Our life stories have somehow become part of the larger story that God has been telling since the beginning of time, his message of hope and recovery.

179

Becoming messengers of God's plan has had an amazing impact upon our lives. The pain of our losses has not been taken away. In fact, sharing with others requires us to re-live the darkest periods of our lives. But pain experienced in the context of encouraging others helps us to transform our losses in order to help God accomplish his higher purpose.

Joanne Jozefowski is the author of a book entitled *The Phoenix Phenomenon: Rising From The Ashes of Grief.* She points out that some people get through the death of loved ones and successfully re-stabilize their lives. Others go on to become phoenix grievers and use their losses to achieve personal development, well beyond the level of growth they had achieved prior to the loss. They transcend and transform the experience of loss to achieve a kind of self-actualization. Many of them go on to work with others who are experiencing losses.

The phenomenon she describes is replicated in those who recover from substance abuse, physical disability, mental illness and the full spectrum of negative life experiences. Phoenix grievers, and others like them, work their losses together for good. They achieve strength out of their weakness and victory out of defeat.

And they have one other essential ingredient to offer others. They have the legitimacy of a wounded healer. They have the answer to the question that many suffering people ask. "Who are you to offer me hope? How do you know what it's like to go through what I am dealing with right now?" It is the legitimacy that God achieved by sending himself in the form of his Son to live among us, die a criminal's death and rise to achieve victory and everlasting life. The good news that is interspersed throughout the New Testament is that when we suffer trials and temptation, we become partners with Christ in his suffering and death.

The irony of becoming messengers of God's plan for healing our losses is that we have to be willing to enter into the death of ourselves. Whether or not we have really understood this essential aspect of our faith, it has been in plain sight throughout the scriptures. The writers of the New Testament, and particularly those that record the words of Jesus, speak of the need to die in order to be transformed into Christ-likeness. The difference between surviving losses in our lives and transforming them into something that can be used as part of God's master plan, seems to me to depend on our willingness to choose God, hold onto hope, and let those deaths occur.

So, what has to die in us in order for us to live in Christ? I do not claim to be an expert in this deep theological mystery, but we have experienced many deaths along the journey that has been thrust upon us. First came the death of a sense of invulnerability—the idea that bad things only happen to other people. Then came the death of a god who always protected us from physical harm and sheltered us from tragedy. We struggled with the contradiction that God allowed tragedy to crash into our lives while at the same time he loved and comforted us through so many different people. Another death came as we gave up our sense of what was normal and struggled to adapt to a new normal. Close behind came the death of self-sufficiency, the idea that we could personally manage our way out of tragedy without the help of others. I had to die to the notion that I am the master of my fate and controller of my destiny.

Each of these deaths has been painful and disturbing, but our association with others who have experienced similar losses has assured us that we are by no means alone. Each death has paved the way for new life and opportunities. The death of invulnerability has given way to a new appreciation for each day we have been given to live and love. The death of our genie god has opened us to the deep compassion of our God who comes alongside us in our suffering and assures us of his love. Our new normal is much closer to the reality that all of us

181

eventually must learn to accept. The death of self-suffi-ciency has opened us to the kindness of friends and com-plete strangers who have been the bearers of God's amazing grace.

So then, if not tragedies of all shapes and sizes, what can separate us from his love, grace, and the fulfillment of his plan? Paul wraps up the powerful eighth chapter of Romans answering with one word. **Nothing**. Nothing can stop his victorious loving march through history. We have that assurance no matter what terrible news we see when we pick up the paper or turn on the television; no matter what happens to us or our family; no matter what dark-ness may come into our lives. Even when we stubbornly refuse to let him into our lives, he waits patiently for us to turn home. Satan keeps dishing out tragedy, condemna-tion, temptation, and heartache, and God trumps Satan with forgiveness, mercy, hope, and most importantly, love.

So, life goes on for us and those God has placed in our lives. We continue to experience all the peaks and valleys that come to all of us if we live long enough. But we expe-rience it with a confidence and blessed assurance that God is our very near and constant companion. And we know that we have joined him in the writing and telling of **the rest of his story.**

Lessons Learned
Looking back on the totality of our experiences has led us to draw some conclusions about how to not only sur-

vive but to transform our wilderness experiences. As time has passed and God has helped to redeem our losses, I can more clearly see how he is using those experiences to advance his master plan. I pray that this book will be part of that process. If I have been successful, many others will use our tragedies to learn to navigate through their own wilderness experiences and learn to transform those painful circumstances. What follows is what I have discovered about what God seems to be up to when we deal with tragedies.

God does not always protect us from harm. A relationship with him is not an insurance policy that protects us from bad things happening to us. But that does not keep us from believing that he is supposed to do just that. When tragedy strikes, a big part of what we must do is to jettison our old beliefs about how God does and does not act. This opens us up to how he is acting in our circumstances. If we refuse to change our view of God, we become angry, embittered, and disappointed. We then lose access to the most important resource we have to recovery.

The fact that God allows suffering in our lives does not mean that he does not love us. It also does not mean that his plan for our lives is off course. He has promised to work all things together for good if we love him and continue to seek him through good times and bad. He has a plan for how to use our experiences, and it may be very different from our own plan for our lives.

God can use our wilderness experiences to accomplish his kingdom work. Suffering softens us and makes us more sensitive to the needs of others who are experiencing

183

hardships. We will discover that we have legitimacy in the lives of others that we did not have prior to our wilderness walk. When we see others suffering, the Spirit draws us to them. Their knowing that we have survived our tragedies with faith and hope intact becomes a connective lifeline to them in the storm.

When tragedy comes our way, it changes our lives forever. We will not emerge from the wilderness as the same person we were when we entered. We have to learn to let our dreams die, but we do not have to give up on hope and faith. When we turn to him in faith and ask for him to teach us, he will respond in his time.

God has a wonderful master plan to use every hardship, every tear, to accomplish his kingdom work. When we consent to be transformed by our suffering and ask God to use us, we enter into the great mystery of the suffering servant. We do not find absolute certainty here. Instead we become more comfortable with the mystery and increasingly confident in the belief that he will disclose to us how he wants to use us in his service. Each new trip into the wilderness is another opportunity to learn about ourselves and God's true nature.

There we discover how our suffering can be used in service of his greater purposes.

There is no more meaningful and fulfilling service than this: knowing how our little stories fit into his big picture and then following his call on our lives.

EPILOGUE

In the process of writing this book our lives have continued to unfold. Some parts have been beautiful and nothing short of miraculous and other parts have been difficult. Knowing that this Epilogue will be out of date almost as soon as I finish it, here are some of the happenings in our family for those who are interested.

Dwayne is now retired and has taken up the challenge of the Appalachian Trail. Tiffany is a very successful and popular hair stylist for men in the west end of Richmond. They divorced a few years ago. Tiffany successfully manages her ulcerative colitis. We are immensely proud of their sons Maxwell and Nicholas. Max graduated from Virginia Military Institute and is serving his county as an officer in the Army. He is stationed in Alaska and has completed one tour in Afghanistan. He proposed to his girlfriend in Italy.

Nic got caught up in the substance abuse epidemic but the signs are that he is breaking free and learning from his mistakes. He will soon have a trade in brick masonry, and more importantly he will have the capacity to help others who are struggling with this pandemic disease of substance abuse.

Jamie has his Masters of Science in Healthcare Administration, and his wife Johnna has her degree in Dental Hygiene. They have a son named Elliott (Eli) Russell Deans. Jamie manages three outpatient clinics for Virginia Commonwealth University Healthcare System. He has a wonderful gift working with those who are dealing with mental illness and is a great trainer as well. Johnna works for a dental practice in the west end of Richmond. They are a loving, giving couple, and they are bringing Eli up in that tradition.

186   Matthew has a Masters in Rehabilitation Counseling Services and works for the Virginia Department of Aging and Rehabilitative Services as a certified Vocational Rehabilitation Counselor. He competes locally and nationally in adaptive sports and has coached wheelchair basketball for kids. He is an inspiration to many, both on and off the job. Ashlee has her undergraduate degree from Radford, and she also works for the VDARS. They gave birth to a beautiful son named Forrest Benson Deans. Given Matthew's injury, Forrest is indeed a miracle child. He loves dinosaurs and like the other Forrest you may have seen on the big screen, he can run like the wind.

Mark remains in successful recovery and is known for his deep wisdom and steadfast support to family and friends. He is working as a superintendent for a commercial construction firm based in Richmond. He is divorced from his first wife, but hope springs eternal, and he is currently dating a beautiful woman who seems to be a wonderful companion for him.

Family relationships for us, as with most everyone, have been sometimes beautiful and sometimes challenging. Some of our children have experienced divorce, and several have been caught up in the difficulties and consequences of substance abuse. We all live within forty-five minutes of one another. We get together frequently and love each other deeply. I know that Shantel would be overjoyed with how we hug each other whenever we get together. Our family is known for its love, and we have produced some of the best huggers in the world. I like to say that when you get hugged by us you get hugged to the bone.

Patsi and I have grown closer with each passing year. She is a professional quilter and accomplished quilt teacher. More importantly she is a life teacher and shares her wisdom with everyone she touches. She is a good friend to many and I am proud to say that I am her best friend.

I am still surviving and still fighting a relentless prostate cancer and the side effects of treatment. But I am an active member of the Us Too prostate cancer support group which meets monthly in Richmond. I have served on the board of directors of Us Too International which supports thousands of prostate cancer warriors throughout the world. I am inclined to say that one day this cancer may take me out of the picture. If not cancer, then something else surely will. But it is **Not This Day.** Today I have another opportunity to live, to learn, to love, and to make a difference in this world.

I am co-leader of a weekly Centering Prayer Group at Richmond Hill, a group that brings great joy and peace

187

to my life. Our group consists of a widely diverse bunch of loving people from different faith backgrounds young and old, inner city kids and accomplished professionals all seeking to surrender themselves to the wonderful mystery of God.

Patsi and I continue to lead a grief support group and help people learn the lessons of grief and loss that were passed down to us many years ago. We are quick to enter the painful and tragic places in peoples' lives with a message of hope and an assurance that with God's help they can survive, overcome and transform their circumstances to help others.

I am praying for those of you who find your way to this book. Our stories seem to resonate with a wide variety of people: cancer survivors, the homeless, families struggling with substance abuse, illness, injury, and loss of loved ones. I believe God has chosen us to share these stories and what he has taught us as we have learned to walk through the wilderness. Wherever you are in your walk I can assure you that you are not privileged nor are you inoculated from tragedy. But you are also not alone. You may be lost and confused but you are not forgotten. The wilderness is indeed much closer than we think. Our lives can turn tragic in the blink of an eye. But God with his immense love and vast resources is closer still.

To finalize the writing of this book, I spoke to those whose names I mention in the stories to get their permission. Many of them talked about what drew them to us when we were going through our time of need. Some said it was a God thing that brought them to our aide, many credited the Holy Spirit in drawing them and others to us and it was a joy to get caught up in it.

One person said that he felt an *irresistible pull* to come along side of us and provide help and friendship without trying to explain why we were dealing with such hardship. So, I close with this. Never count God out of the picture no matter your circumstances. Keep praying; keep asking for prayer and let the hardships in your life soften you to the hurting and suffering that is happening all around us. Above all, stay open to the mysterious irresistible pull of the Holy Spirit on your life to reach out to others who are hurting. By doing so you are transforming your life with all its hurts and hardships and becoming part of God's Master Plan.

May God bless you and yours.
Jerry and Patsi Deans.
February 28th, 2019

authorjerrydeans@gmail.com

Made in the USA
Monee, IL
09 January 2021